Demystifying Job Development

Field-Based Approaches to Job Development for People with Disabilities

David Hoff, Cecilia Gandolfo, Marty Gold, and Melanie Jordan

Institute for Community Inclusion/UAP

Children's Hospital and University of Massachusetts/Boston

Training Resource Network, Inc. ● St. Augustine, Florida

First Edition

This publication is sold with the understanding that the publisher is not engaged in rendering legal, financial, medical, or other such services. If legal advice or other such expert assistance is required, a competent professional in the appropriate field should be sought. All brand and product names are trademarks or registered trademarks of their respective companies.

Printed in the United States of America.

Published by Training Resource Network, Inc., PO Box 439, St. Augustine, FL 32085-0439; www.trninc.com.

Library of Congress Cataloging-in-Publication Data
Demystifying job development : field-based approaches to job development for people with disabilities / David Hoff ... [et al.].-- 1st ed.
    p. cm.
    ISBN 1-883302-37-4
    1. Rehabilitation counseling. 2. Rehabilitation counselors--Training of. 3. Vocational Guidance for the handicapped--Study and teaching. 4. Handicapped--Employment. 5. Job hunting. 6. Job creation. I. Hoff, David, date.

HD7255.5 .D455 2000
362.4'0484--dc21

00-029890

Table of Contents

Exercises

Acknowledgments

Our thanks to our colleagues at the Institute for Community Inclusion, Margaret Van Gelder, Joseph Marrone, Cindy Thomas, John Butterworth, Sheila Fesko and the Institute's director, William Kiernan, for their support and contributions in the development of this book.

Also, thank you to Ellen Ball Nalven, the director of employment services at Our House, Inc., in Berkeley Heights, New Jersey, on whose work and ideas much of the material on situational assessment is based, and who is a shining example of excellence in our field.

Finally, a special acknowledgment and thanks to all the many people with disabilities who we have had the wonderful opportunity to work with over the years, and assist in making their employment dreams become a reality. They truly have been our teachers and our inspiration.

Introduction

Successful job development starts with a firmly held set of values regarding people with disabilities. These values shape agency and program goals and practices, including the approach to job development. Employment in our society is key not only for providing the means to obtain material goods. It is also a fundamental component of participation in society. Work is the basis for many relationships and experiences in life. People with disabilities must be viewed as having both the rights and responsibilities of being employed in the community.

Given the right job and supports, all people with disabilities can work. This statement is not meant to make light of the inherent difficulties in helping people with disabilities get and keep jobs. Experience has shown, however, that it is impossible to accurately determine who can and cannot succeed in community employment based on any sort of so-called "objective evaluation."

It is time to stop asking the questions, "Can this person work?" and "Is he or she work ready?" Instead, start with the assumption that everyone is "work ready" and that it is a matter of finding the right opportunity and supports to enable each person to work successfully.

Given this, the goal of community rehabilitation programs (and the task for job developers) is not to decide whether people can or should work, but simply to help people with disabilities get and keep jobs. This entails working with individuals to identify their interests and skills and working with employers to identify and advocate for employment opportunities. The challenge is to use all the skills, expertise, connections, and creativity we collectively possess to translate our values into practices that enable people with the most severe disabilities to work successfully in the community.

Why "Demystifying Job Development"?

The methods used in helping vocational professionals become comfortable and competent in developing jobs need a fresh approach. Despite relevant materials, interesting presentations, and positive evaluations, job development training seems to have little impact on what staff do once they return to their jobs. Even when staff members have the information, many still feel hesitant to go out and contact employers and may avoid doing so. As a result, the concept of "Demystifying Job Development" was born, based on the following premises:

- You already possess many of the skills and strategies needed to develop jobs.
- This manual will help you identify your strengths and skills and begin to apply these to your work.
- You need to build your self confidence, so you can devote more time to job development.
- Job development is best learned by doing, not listening.
- The best place to do job development is out in the community.

About the Manual

The goals for this manual are threefold: to teach specific job development skills and strategies, to increase self-confidence in doing job development, and to help you do more and better job development. It can be self-paced or used in staff training.

The manual is divided into sections that roughly follow the process of developing a job for an individual. It starts with the basic values and approaches to assisting individuals with severe disabilities in identifying their interests and skills. It then translates this into a plan for finding a job.

Next, strategies for making contacts with employers, ways to present and market job seekers, and specific approaches to identifying job opportunities for individuals who need very specialized job placements are covered. Then we look at methods for negotiating with employers and developing and maintaining relationships.

The final section presents strategies that job developers can use to prioritize and use their time effectively in developing jobs, along with suggestions for ongoing professional development.

THE 10 COMMANDMENTS OF JOB DEVELOPMENT

Thou Shalt:

- *Convince people that work is productive, healthy, and beneficial.*

- *Assist people who are considered not "job ready" to find and keep jobs.*

- *Help people explore their interests and get jobs based on their interests.*

- *Use an individualized approach to working with each person.*

- *Give people your best professional advice, but respect individuals' choices.*

- *Advocate for opportunities for people within your own agencies, with other agencies, families, and employers.*

- *Never provide information or job leads without direct support, and follow-up by you.*

- *Provide different (unequal) levels of support to each individual.*

- *Give people many chances to succeed (and support and motivate people when they don't succeed).*

- *Make job development a priority in how you allocate your time weekly.*

1

A Person-Centered Approach to Job Development

This section provides the core strategies for successful placement of individuals with severe disabilities in quality jobs in the community. This approach to employment highlights social inclusion and the use of natural community and workplace supports as essential elements for both getting a job (career exploration, job development, and support planning) and maintaining employment.

A person-centered approach starts with focusing on what the person wants to and can do now, rather than determining what he or she has to change to become "job ready." Though this approach may seem unrealistic or naive to some, there is no simple criterion or characteristic that predicts who can or can't work successfully. And particularly for people with more severe disabilities, getting individuals ready for employment through pre-vocational and vocational training in day habilitation programs, adult training centers, day treatment programs, and sheltered workshops has not met with a high degree of success.

The failure of this readiness model has led to the development of strategies such as transitional employment (for people with mental illness) and supported employment. Both share the common philosophy that the best place for people with disabilities to learn to work is on the job, with an array of supports available to help each worker be successful. The presumption used in this manual is that once people are done with their formal education, they are as "job ready" for the most part as they are going to be, and work must proceed from there.

While it probably wouldn't hurt any of us to embark on a program of personal self-improvement, such a need does not stop people without disabilities from becoming employed, nor should it stop people with disabilities. As Gerry Provencal said, "We're far too patient with the passage of time for people with disabilities. Time is as precious for a person with a disability as it is for all of us."

Person-Centered Planning

To assist the individual job seeker in determining his or her interests and skills, this book uses a person-centered planning approach combined with creative brainstorming and actual experiences in the community as the basis for developing a career direction and early job development activities. Person-centered planning is covered only briefly. But understanding this philosophy and some of the basic techniques is an essential part of finding quality employment opportunities in the community for job seekers with disabilities.

The use of person-centered planning has taken on the aura of a "mystic process" that requires a high degree of skill, following distinctly prescribed methodologies and formats. However, the emphasis here is not on methodology, but rather on the importance of adopting a person-centered philosophy throughout the job development and placement process.

The essence of a person-centered planning approach is to help a person identify personal desires and start taking steps to achieve his or her desires and dreams through employment. It includes reaching out to family, friends, and community resources to help generate career directions, employment contacts, and supports.

- consumer
- family and friends
- residential staff
- other agency staff
- community leaders
- employers and businesses
- funding agency

Understanding the preferences and needs of the individual also includes understanding the culture and values of the person, the family, and the community. Most important, but most difficult to do, is to look beyond what has been achieved thus far and not to be deterred by past failures or uncertainty of future success. Person-centered planning is nothing more than good planning, which involves developing solutions that meet the needs of an individual through collaboration, creative thought, and problem solving.

Brainstorming

This approach requires "taking off the blinders" and considering a much wider range of possibilities. Creative brainstorming techniques can help do just that. Look beyond the usual cast of characters such as agency employment staff and the job seeker. Invite other agency staff, the board of directors, family members, friends, employers, and other community members. For example, receptionists, maintenance people, and bookkeepers often have both good ideas and extensive personal contacts.

The possibilities are endless. People who can provide a variety of perspectives and ideas about possible career directions and who can help make contacts within the business community are needed. For creative brainstorming to work, it should be incorporated as a normal part of how an organization operates. For example, information and ideas can be gathered from a variety of sources at the beginning of the job development process. Or, you can set aside time at every staff or Business Advisory Council meeting for a brainstorming session to identify interests, skills, potential jobs, and contacts for one individual served by the program.

Using groups of people to brainstorm ideas and strategies for jobs is an integral component of a person-centered planning approach. Involving a wide variety of individuals in the process not only leads to a better quality process and outcomes. It also helps job developers use their time more efficiently in a streamlined job development process.

What a person is interested in is strongly influenced by what he or she has experienced in life. The reality for many people with disabilities is that their life experiences have been very limited. So, part of a good planning process involves providing real opportunities to enable individuals to make more informed choices. Techniques such as informational interviewing, workplace tours, and situational assessments get useful information about the person in a quick and cost efficient manner. This allows you to move quickly into actual job development.

The information gathered not only identifies specific interests and skills. It also highlights personal characteristics and other attributes the job seeker has to offer and what work environments and work culture will fit best.

BRAINSTORMING BASICS

- Generate lots of ideas.
- Involve anyone and everyone.
- Get different perspectives.
- There is no wrong answer.
- All ideas are valid.
- Search for different questions.

There are two extremes that can occur in this process. In one, no planning occurs. This results in a chaotic job search, with no rational course of action, that ends either in a poor job match or no job at all. The other is an excessive amount of planning, which delays the job search and disillusions everyone involved (particularly the job seeker). Each individual who is looking for a job should have a simple plan in place that is reviewed and revised every thirty days until the person is successfully employed.

PROBLEM SOLVING STEPS

1. Decide whom to involve.
2. Fact finding – no assumptions!
3. Define the problem.
4. Generate alternative solutions.
5. Investigate – everyone helps!
6. Choose an alternative.
7. Try it out!
8. Evaluate the results.
9. If necessary try something else.

Have you ever had a certain impression about what a field of work or job was like, only to have that impression change significantly once you worked in that field or explored it more closely? People with disabilities are like anyone else. They verbally may express an interest in a field, but have a limited understanding of what the particular line of work entails. Additionally, they may have a finite view of the types of employment that are available.

The following methods can help determine the types of positions to explore as part of the actual job development process.

- **Informational Interviewing**
  Informational interviewing involves meeting with an employer, not for a job interview, but simply to gather information about the business. It is a wonderful technique for career exploration and for helping job seekers (and job developers) gain experience in interacting with employers without the pressure of an interview focused on a hiring decision.

- **Job Tours**
  Similar to informational interviewing, touring various businesses can be useful in exposing the job seeker and job developer to a variety of businesses as part of a career exploration process.

- **Job Shadowing**
  Job shadowing involves spending time observing an individual performing a job. This can be for a short period of time, the entire work day, or a series of days, depending on the nature of the job and level of interest of the job seeker.

- **Community Exploration**
  Particularly for individuals who have trouble verbally expressing their preferences, spending time in the community with the job developer, going into various businesses, and just observing sometimes can help determine where a job seeker's interests and preferences lie.

- **Community and Business Research**
  As part of the job development planning process, it can be helpful to do some research on the local business community and economy to get a handle on what types of jobs are available (and not available), areas of growth, and who the biggest employers are. Such information is available from US Bureau of Labor Statistics (www.bls.gov/ro1con.htm) as well as state, county, and local economic development offices. In addition, research on specific employers also can be helpful in planning job development and identifying business contacts. Sources for such information include annual reports, business publications, newspapers, and information packets from the employer. The advent of the world wide web has made collecting such information much easier. This is a good starting point.

- **One-Stop Centers**
  One-Stop Centers are publicly funded facilities to assist all job seekers to find employment. One-Stops have a variety of materials and services to explore possible jobs and careers, available at no charge. A nationwide listing of One-Stop Centers is available from the US Department of Labor, Employment and Training Administration web site at www.ttrc.doleta.gov/ETA. You also can contact your state or county department of labor or employment. When searching for locations of One-Stops, keep in mind that the centers often do not have One-Stop as part of their name (e.g., centers in New Hampshire are called New Hampshire Works, and in Massachusetts the centers go by a variety of names).

- **Volunteer Work**

  For some individuals, and for certain areas of employment, doing volunteer work may be a helpful step as part of the career planning process. For example, many people are first attracted to the human service field as a result of volunteer work. Similarly, many people enter radio and television production work through volunteer work and internships. From a values standpoint though, it is important to recognize that volunteer work is not a substitute for paid employment. Also, from both from a legal and ethical standpoint, people with disabilities should do only volunteer work that is similar to what other members of the community are doing as volunteers. Additionally, it sometimes can take enormous effort to find a volunteer job for a person with a significant disability. Such effort might be better spent on finding paid employment. Volunteer work is an option for some people in specific situations, but it is not for everyone.

- **Taking a Class**

  Taking classes in an adult education program or at a community college can be a way of finding out a job seeker's interest and aptitude in a field.

- **Situational Assessment**

  Situational assessment is trying out a job in the community, for a few hours up to a few days, so the job seeker can determine if he or she is well-suited for that type of work.

The methods used for career exploration vary, depending on the needs and abilities of the individual. There is no one right formula for every individual. Keep in mind the following considerations:

- Choose methods that are appropriate to the individual. For example, someone with limited interpersonal communication skills and abilities probably is not going to benefit from an informational interview and possibly would be better off doing a situational assessment.
- Use methods that provide the greatest amount of information in the quickest fashion, in order to move ahead with the actual job search. Methods such as taking a class or doing volunteer work can take an extensive amount of time. The job seeker should use them only if there is a clear rationale for it, or if the individual is already working and they are part of a career progression strategy.
- Keep in mind that the purpose is to gather enough information to move ahead with the job search, not spend a lifetime researching and exploring various jobs and careers. Don't let excessive career exploration become an excuse for not moving ahead on job development.

No matter what methods you use as part of the career exploration process, it's important to gather certain information as part of this process. Look for these two categories of information:

1) types of work and skill requirements of jobs that the job seeker is interested in;

2) the types of work cultures and work environments that an individual is comfortable in and would like to work in.

Job development for people with disabilities too often tends to focus exclusively on what task skills the individual has. Yet many people (with and without disabilities) succeed or fail on a job based on how well they fit into the social environment of the workplace. In developing successful employment opportunities, the job developer and job seeker need to consider in which work environments an individual's personality would be considered a real asset (e.g., a friendly, outgoing personality is an important attribute for a customer service job, while a quiet personality might be good for someone doing data entry).

As career exploration progresses, the job developer and job seeker should look for common themes among areas of interest. For example, one individual explored several different fields. She had an interest in a variety of jobs. But the ones she was most intrigued by were jobs with a great deal of interaction with others, a low level of supervision, an informal work atmosphere, and a variety of tasks.

The following is a list of areas to consider in a job or career exploration process. Examine this information from two perspectives:

1) the criteria or requirements of a field or specific job in each of these areas;

2) the comfort level or ability of the job seeker to meet these requirements.

- formality or informality of workplace
- amount of supervision
- level of interaction with co-workers and supervisors
- camaraderie and socialization of employees
- level of worker autonomy
- variety of tasks
- training required
- stamina and endurance
- mobility requirements
- communication
- production rate
- strength: lifting and carrying
- manual dexterity
- reading requirements
- mathematics/counting
- level of independence required
- customer contact
- dress requirements
- need to work independently
- flexibility and changes in routine
- complexity of tasks
- repetitive nature of tasks
- amount of self-initiative required
- need/ability to tell time and time awareness
- stress and pressure of position
- need to ask for assistance
- area orientation requirements
- environment: noise, temperature, indoors/outdoors

Situational Assessment

Situational assessment is a valuable tool for assisting a person with a disability to make choices about the types of jobs and work environments he or she enjoys. Also known as job sampling, on-the-job assessment, or environmental assessment, it uses actual employment and community settings.

Assessments in simulated work environments and facility-based programs such as sheltered workshops simply do not contain the various nuances and variables of actual work environments. These are necessary to make an educated choice concerning employment options.

Through situational assessment, the job seeker is given real choice through exposure to a variety of work environments. He or she is not forced to rely on the "expert" opinion of professionals or family members concerning what kind of work is and is not appropriate. The job seeker and job devel-

oper are able to learn about the complete reality of the work environment, including task skill requirements, variety of tasks and activities on the job, social skill requirements, formality level, pace of activity, amount of personal interaction, and the comfort level of the job seeker with different environments.

Sometimes the job seeker and job developer spend enormous time and energy pursuing a specific type of job based on very limited information of that particular field of work. If and when a job finally is secured, the job may be a poor match. Situational assessment lets you generate information quickly about employment options that are worth pursuing. This avoids wasting time on inappropriate job searches.

Situational assessment reduces the risk to both the job seeker and the employer in the placement process. Particularly for job seekers who are somewhat ambivalent or concerned about working in the community, situational assessment expands their exposure to the community in a low-risk way. One of the criticisms of more traditional assessment techniques is that they evaluate work skills that have limited application in today's workplace. Through situational assessment, you assess skills that are used in actual work environments.

You also more readily can identify the availability of supports and support needs through situational assessment. It allows for evaluation of an individual's support needs in an actual work environment, as well as the ability of the work environment to "naturally" provide those work supports.

Situational assessment also helps to deal with the issue of so-called "job readiness." A major barrier for placement of people with disabilities into employment often has been the determination by experts that the individual isn't "ready" to work in the community due to behavioral issues, lack of motivation, or other issues.

Yet experience has shown that when an individual is in a "real" work environment in the community, issues considered to be a barrier to employment turn out to be non-issues. For example, behavior that is considered "inappropriate" in a facility-based program may be perfectly appropriate for a work environment in the community, or the change in environment may cause the behavior to diminish or disappear.

Like any tool, situational assessment should be used in a sensitive manner, based on individual job seeker needs. For people with extensive work histories, and for those whose job goals have become clear through more traditional methods, situational assessment is not necessary or appropriate. However, situational assessment is helpful for individuals with little or no work experience, difficulties with communication, or unclear job goals.

Paying the Job Seeker for Assessments

A major question concerning situational assessment is payment of individuals for the tasks they perform as part of the assessment process. Job seekers should be paid for assessments. Simply put, people should be paid for working.

However, US Department of Labor regulations do allow, under specific guidelines, for assessments to occur without payment. (State and local laws may be more restrictive.) The guidelines for non-paid assessments are at the end of this chapter.

Beyond the values issues, there are a number of other concerns about nonpayment of individuals for assessments. Not paying individuals for a situational assessment can change the dynamics of the assessment, since the impact of working for pay cannot be evaluated.

The flexibility of the assessment also is limited by the restrictions of non-paid assessments, in which you must track information to ensure that regulations are followed. Paying individuals not only makes sense from a values standpoint, but makes doing the assessment a much simpler and straightforward process.

Paying individuals obviously requires identifying a source of payment. There may be some flexible funding available within your program for such activities. If not, check with your current funding agency for possible options.

Situational assessment is also the type of service that private foundations and civic organizations are willing to fund, particularly since the funds go directly to individuals with disabilities and the goal of such funding is straightforward (providing funding will lead to employment in the community).

Some programs have had success having employers pay for short-term assessments. This is worth pursuing, but there are some considerations:

- When an assessment is not employer-paid, setting it up can be a fairly simple process, because all you are asking for is use of the employer's facility. When the assessment is employer-paid, it can complicate and lengthen the process. It may take as much time and energy to set up an employer-paid assessment as it does to actually get an individual hired. The idea is to possibly set up a number of assessments in fairly quick fashion. If it takes several weeks to set up each assessment, it is counterproductive to an efficient job-development process.
- Another issue with assessments being employer-paid is that it potentially changes the nature of the assessment. When employers are paying for the assessment, they will expect the individual to be productive. The purpose here is to assess the person's ability to perform a variety of tasks. Being productive to the employer's benefit is a secondary consideration.

Insurance Coverage

Hopefully everything will go wonderfully with the assessment, but unforeseen events do occur. Therefore, insurance coverage is another issue to consider with situational assessment.

There are two types of coverage a program should have: worker's compensation, if the worker with a disability should be injured during the course of the assessment; and liability, in case the worker with a disability damages employer's equipment or property during the course of the assessment. (One advantage to an employer-paid assessment is that insurance coverage is not an issue, since the individual is covered under the employer's policies.)

On the surface, these seem like complex issues to be resolved. But this is usually fairly simple to deal with. Typically a conversation with your agency's insurance agent, and possibly the addition of a rider on your policy for a relatively small fee, is all that is needed. Speak to whoever handles arranging insurance coverage in your agency.

Identifying Assessment Sites

In identifying assessment sites, start with the job seeker's preferences. What kind of jobs has he or she expressed interest in? What kind of ideas have been generated through the planning process that need further exploration?

However, don't be limited by the expressed interests of the job seeker. Remember, part of the purpose here is to expand the horizons of the job seeker. Look for other work environments that might provide further information on the person's preferences and alternative choices.

The next step involves contacting employers to arrange situational assessments. Future chapters offer details about contacting employers and developing employer relationships for job placements. Similar methods, such as networking and cold calls, can be used to set up situational assessments.

However, contacting employers to set up situational assessments is considerably simpler than job development for actual placements, since the commitment you are asking from the employer is relatively small: the use of their facility, and a little bit of their time and cooperation.

For example, let's say you are working with someone who is interested in music. Among the ideas that have been identified is working in a recording studio. You contact a studio and say, "I'm working with an individual who is interested in possibly working in a recording studio. At this point, we're still identifying what tasks he could do in this type of environment. If possible, I would like to bring him in, to not only see your facilities and what you do, but to give him the opportunity to try out various jobs and tasks in the studio. Our agency would pay the individual for performing this work, and there would be no cost to you." From there, it would be a matter of negotiating the specifics of the assessment.

The following are basic guidelines for what to cover when meeting with employers concerning setting up a situational assessment.

- Give a brief description of your agency and the job seekers you represent.
- Give an overview of what situational assessment is, and the advantages of using actual work environments for assessment.
- Learn about their business - what they do and how they do it
- Through your discussions with the employer and tour of the workplace, identify specific areas and tasks to be part of the assessment process
- Be very clear about the parameters of the assessment – that the purpose is for evaluation, not to be extra help for the employer.
- Emphasize the value you place on not inconveniencing the employer when situational as-

sessments occur (i.e., you recognize they have a business to run). Assure the employer about staff availability, professionalism, and responsiveness.
- Solicit and respond to concerns.
- Discuss specifics of setting up an assessment.
- Provide written materials that reemphasize items discussed.

You already may have contacts and opportunities within your organization that can be used to set up assessment sites. These include:
- Using employers whom you previously contacted that had no current job openings, but seemed open to the possibility of hiring a worker with a disability.
- Using sites in which you already have individuals working. If your agency has enclaves or transitional employment, this simply involves adding an extra person. However, in cases where people are working in individual placements (which is hopefully the vast majority of the people served by your agency), this should be done with caution. If the person works for a large employer, with departments or sites that are separate from the person who already works there, this may be an option. However, the assessment should not occur side-by-side, or near the person with a disability who is employed there.

A good practice during job development, when it is clear that there are no immediate employment prospects, is to ask about using the employer's workplace for assessment. This can be a great way to develop relationships with employers over the long-term, gradually creating understanding of the capabilities of people with disabilities. Often the use of an employer as an assessment site over an extended period of time has led to the development of actual placements with that employer.

In developing assessment sites, two approaches are useful. One is to identify sites for onetime use by a specific individual. The other is to develop a number of sites, which can be used on a periodic basis, with assessments set up with a few days' notice. This typically can be set up through informal agreements with employers (i.e., "We'll give you a call a few days ahead of time, to let you know when someone is coming in for an assessment."). Having a number of sites prearranged can speed up the assessment process, rather than having to develop various sites for each individual you serve.

However, if an individual has a specific interest for which an assessment site does not exist, you should arrange a new site. Telling a consumer "Sorry, we don't have an assessment site in that kind of job" is no excuse. It's important to have different types of employers available to use for assessment that represent the diversity of interests of job seekers and the wide array of employment opportunities available in the community.

The employers should be both traditional (e.g., retail, food service, janitorial) and nontraditional. It also can be helpful to have assessment sites with similar tasks but different work environments, in order to see the impact of different environments. For example, clerical work in a small office that employs twenty people is a very different experience from a large corporate employer with 2,000 employees.

Finally, it's important not to "burn out" employers. Part of the discussion with businesses in arranging assessments should be about how often they are comfortable with your using their work site for assessment. Agencies should be careful of not using the same assessment sites too often, both to provide more diverse assessment experiences for job seekers and to maintain positive business relationships.

Length of the Assessment

The length of the assessment will be very dependent on the individuals involved. In some cases, a few hours may be enough to provide sufficient information about a specific type of job, or may be all that an individual has the energy or tolerance for. In other cases, several days at the same job site may be appropriate.

The decision ultimately should come down to determining the length of time it will take to gather sufficient information to make a decision about whether or not to move forward with job development in this particular type of work. In some cases it may be necessary and worthwhile to do an assessment at the same site several times, to allow the person an opportunity to get used to the work environment and tasks.

Number of Assessments

Similar to the *length* of assessments, the *number* of assessments will be dependent on the individual. For people who have a pretty clear idea of what they want to do, a few assessments can con-

firm the direction to go in and provide some more specific information about areas for job development. For people who are unsure about what types of jobs they are interested in, or if it is not clear what direction to go in, many different assessments might be necessary, at a wide variety of employment sites.

Doing the Assessment

The following are some basic assessment guidelines:

- Agency staff presence during the assessment is dependent on the individuals involved in the assessment and the employer. In general, the rule should be to err on the side of too much staff presence rather than too little, particularly with newer assessment sites. There are cases in which the individual is fairly independent and may not be comfortable with ongoing staff presence. Or, it may be stigmatizing. In those cases, lessen staff presence. You also may have assessment sites where there is a well-established relationship with the employer, and supervisors and coworkers feel comfortable being more involved in the assessment, handling issues that may arise.
- Ask the employer ahead of time about how staff will be informed about the assessment, and how you may assist in creating understanding and comfort with what is occurring.
- Make sure the job seeker is dressed appropriately for the work environment and is well aware of the purpose of the assessment.
- Ensure that the job seeker performs a variety of jobs and tasks within the work environment.
- Use some type of standardized tool to collect information so that a comprehensive assessment occurs; make sure the assessment includes evaluation of job skills, as well social and workplace culture issues.
- Encourage interaction between the individual with a disability and the employees who are working there.
- Be very conscious throughout the assessment about the work environment; minimize the intrusion into the workplace and avoid creating a distraction.
- At the end of the assessment, get feedback from the job seeker as well as the employer.

Using Situational Assessment Information

Once situational assessments have occurred, the job seeker can discuss the experiences with the job developer and help make decisions about the direction of the job search. Discussion should include such things as: work environments the job seeker liked or disliked and why, tasks he or she did well and enjoyed performing, tasks the job seeker found to be a challenge, what places felt comfortable, and things that were different than expected.

Next, use the information to target specific jobs and employers. The job seeker and the job developer confidently can state to prospective employers that the job seeker has spent time in work environments similar to the prospective job and has demonstrated the ability to perform tasks and jobs within that work environment. For individuals with significant disabilities who require some type of job creation or job carving, situational assessment can be a very useful tool in identifying specific tasks that can be carved out to create a job.

One job seeker did an assessment in an office environment. The results of the assessment indicated she was comfortable in that environment. She could handle sorting of mail to about thirty people and do basic photocopy and filing involving matching documents to file names. However, the assessment showed that complex copy work (multi-page, double-sided documents) and filing that required a high degree of alphabetizing were tasks that went beyond her capabilities. The job developer and job seeker then used the information to identify and create a position that consisted of the tasks the individual did well on.

Situational Assessment as Job Try-Out

So far, we have addressed the use of situational assessment as a major component of the planning and evaluation process prior to job development. However, there is another way that situational assessment can be used: as a job "try out" as part of the hiring decision. In essence, you are offering the employer an opportunity to fully evaluate the individual's ability to perform the tasks of the position, by allowing the individual to try the job for a few hours, a day, or even a couple of days, at no obligation to the employer. If you use situational assessment in this way, the following guidelines are important:

- The parameters of the assessment should be clear to all involved, including the length of the assessment and at what point the hiring decision will be made.
- The person with a disability must be absolutely comfortable with the idea of situational assessment as a job tryout. The benefits of using such a tool should be explained to the job seeker. But if he or she is not comfortable with it, you should not use it.
- When using situational assessment for evaluation purposes, it is helpful to have the involvement of co-workers and supervisors. In the case of a job tryout, however, it is essential. This lets you identify the fit between the individual and the work culture and available supports and be sure the employer has sufficient information to make a hiring decision.
- When using situational assessment as a job try out, explain clearly to the employer that the purpose is to determine whether the individual has the potential to successfully perform in the job over the long-term. The employer should not necessarily expect the individual to have "mastered" the job at the end of the assessment, particularly if he or she has a longer learning curve.

There sometimes are concerns about possibly stigmatizing the person with a disability when situational assessment is used as part of the actual hiring process. The basic concern is expressed as "People without disabilities don't typically have to try out a job before they get hired, so why should people with disabilities have to do so?"

This is a very valid concern. However, consider the criteria that typically are used in hiring: performance in an interview, background and experience, and possibly the results of testing. Using the typical hiring process is always the preferred choice; however, the typical hiring process does not always create awareness by the potential employer about the strengths and abilities of an applicant with a disability.

The reality for many people with disabilities is that the typical criteria are going to exclude them from being hired. Due to physical challenges in communicating, difficulties in verbally articulating their thoughts, or simply lack of experience in interviewing, some people with disabilities perform poorly in interviews. People with disabilities often have limited work experience to demonstrate their ability to perform successfully in the job. Limited academic skills can create challenges in performing on tests. In such cases, you should develop alternative strategies so that people with disabilities can demonstrate to employers that they can perform the tasks of a job they are applying for.

If you are using situational assessment as a job tryout, bear in mind that employers are not simply doing you a favor by allowing its use. Situational assessment as a job tryout should instead be portrayed as a reasonable accommodation of the normal hiring process, under the Americans with Disabilities Act, in order that the job applicant with a disability gets equal consideration.

Job seeking is not just about the business making a decision concerning whether or not to hire a job seeker. The job seeker also needs to make an informed decision about whether he or she wants to work in the type of job being considered and for that particular employer. Situational assessment can provide that type of information.

In deciding whether to use situational assessment as a job tryout, consider the following:

- Can the job seeker properly represent his or her abilities through normal hiring processes of interviewing, testing, and assessment based on past work experience and education?
- How well does the job seeker communicate, interact, and respond to questions?
- Most importantly, what does the job seeker want, and what is he or she comfortable with?

Ultimately, the decision about using situational assessment as a job tryout comes down to the answer to the following question: Will the normal hiring process allow the individual with a disability to receive equal consideration along with other applicants? If not, then a job tryout using situational assessment may be a useful tool.

Department of Labor Regulations for Assessment

STATEMENT OF PRINCIPLE

The US Department of Labor and community-based rehabilitation organizations are committed to the continued development and implementation of individual vocational rehabilitation programs that will facilitate the transition of persons with disabilities into employment within their communities. This transition must take place under conditions that will not jeopardize the protections afforded by the Fair Labor Standards Act to program participants, employees, employers, or other programs providing rehabilitation services to individuals with disabilities.

GUIDELINES

Where ALL of the following criteria are met, the US Department of Labor will NOT assert an employment relationship for purpose of the Fair Labor Standards Act.

- Participants will be individuals with physical and/or mental disabilities for whom competitive employment at or above the minimum wage level is not immediately obtainable and who, because of their disability, will need intensive ongoing support to perform in a work setting.

- Participation will be for vocational exploration, assessment, or training in a community-based placement work site under the general supervision of rehabilitation organization personnel.

- Community-based placements will be clearly defined components of individual rehabilitation programs developed and designed for the benefit of each individual. The statement of needed transition services established for the exploration, assessment, or training components will be included in the person's Individual Written Rehabilitation Plan (IWRP).

- Information contained in the IWRP will not have to be made available. However, documentation as to the individual's enrollment in the community-based placement program will be made available to the

Department of Labor. The individual and, when appropriate, the parent or guardian of each individual must be fully informed of the IWRP and the community-based placement component and have indicated voluntary participation with the understanding that participation in such a component does not entitle the participant to wages.

• The activities of the individuals at the community-based placement site do not result in an immediate advantage to the business. The Department of Labor will look at several factors.

1) There has been no displacement of employees, vacant positions have not been filled, employees have not been relieved of assigned duties, and the individuals are not performing services that, although not ordinarily performed by employees, clearly are of benefit to the business.

2) The individuals are under continued and direct supervision by either representatives of the rehabilitation facility or by employees of the business.

3) Such placements are made according to the requirements of the individual's IWRP and not to meet the labor needs of the business.

4) The periods of time spent by the individuals at any one site or in any clearly distinguishable job classification are specifically limited by the IWRP.

• While the existence of an employment relationship will not be determined exclusively on the basis of the number of hours, as a general rule, each component will not exceed the following limitations:
• Vocational explorations - 5 hours per job experienced
• Vocational assessment - 90 hours per job experienced
• Vocational training - 120 hours per job experienced

• Individuals are not entitled to employment at the business at the conclusion of their IWRP, however, once an individual becomes an employee, the person cannot be considered a trainee at that particular community-based placement unless in a clearly distinguishable occupation.

An employment relationship will exist unless all of the criteria described in the policy is met. If an employment relationship is found to exist, the business will be held responsible for full compliance with the applicable sections of the Fair Labor Standards Act, including those relating to child labor.

Businesses and rehabilitation organizations may, at any time, consider participants to be employees and may structure the program so that the participants are compensated in accordance with the requirements of the Fair Labor Standards Act. Whenever an employment relationship is established, the business may make use of the special minimum wage provisions provided pursuant to section 14(c) of the act.

Questions & Answers
• The criteria in the guidelines indicate that the community-based rehabilitation program is intended for consumers who will need "intensive ongoing support" to perform in a work setting. Does this mean that it is intended for consumers with more severe disabilities?
Community-based vocational programs are intended for those consumers with more severe disabilities. However, the level of severity must be based on skills and behaviors necessary to function in a work setting. Examples of ongoing support services include job redesign, environmental adaptation, personal assistance services, transportation, and social skills training.

• If the activity ordinarily is not performed by the employees and yet is beneficial to the business, can the consumer perform the activity?

The consumer either should not perform the activity or be paid appropriate wages. Although regular employees have not been displaced or relieved of assigned duties, the consumer is still providing services that are of benefit to the business. Therefore, an employment relationship exists between the consumer and the employer. This would not be the case if the activity were of no benefit to the employer and consisted of "busy work" designed to develop or improve a consumer's skills. For example, reorganizing materials awaiting shipment into sets of five would not constitute an employment relationship if the business did not ship materials in this manner.

• What are the implications of the "continued and direct supervision" requirement for agencies and employers?

Direct supervision can include: 1) one-to-one instruction, 2) small group instruction, 3) supervision in close proximity, and 4) supervision in frequent, regular intervals. Supervision in frequent, regular intervals is permitted when the goal is to assess ability to work independently or to demonstrate mastery of the vocational skill.

• What type of documentation is required?

Three types of documentation must be employed to meet the requirements of these guidelines: 1) an IWRP reflecting vocational instruction and training goals and objectives relevant to community-based vocational experience, 2) a letter of agreement outlining the DOL/National Rehabilitation Facilities Coalition agreements listed above and signed by all participants, and 3) ongoing case notes (i.e., attendance records, progress reports).

• What is the distinction between benefit to consumer vs. benefit to employer?

Benefit to the employer occurs when the employer recognizes an immediate advantage by having the consumer working on the premises. An immediate advantage can be described in terms of increased profitability or production for the business. The courts and experts in the field suggest that for the community-based experience to represent a valid experience the following instructional practices should be implemented:

1) Consumers receive adequate orientation and instruction before performing new tasks.
2) The consumer's goals and objectives to be met in the community-based vocational rehabilitation program are clearly defined.
3) Activities in the community-based setting relate directly to the consumer's goals and objectives.
4) The consumer's activities in the community-based vocational rehabilitation program are closely monitored.
5) Records of the consumer's progress are maintained.
6) The necessary support and time for consumers to develop proficiency at new tasks are provided.

• What is the role of the agency in assuring that regular employees will not be displaced by the consumer in the workplace?

The community experience must be primarily for the benefit of the consumer. Also the regular employees must not be displaced or relived of their assigned duties and vacant positions should not go unfilled. Two strategies are available to the rehabilitation organization for ensuring that this criterion is met. First, the agency can confirm that all parties - the employer and the consumer - understand that the consumer must not displace regular employees. An agreement documenting this understanding should be signed by all involved. Secondly, those who provide direct supervision to the consumer at the worksite may observe when employee displacement and other violations are occurring and take steps to correct the situation.

• Do these guidelines from the US Department of Labor supersede individual state departments of labor regulations?

No. It is important that community-based vocational education programs comply with both the US Department of Labor regulations and state department of labor regulations. Where the two do not agree, the regulations with the most stringent requirements for protecting individuals in work settings must apply.

Exercise I-A
Case Study of Jeremy

Purpose: To provide an approach to career exploration and placement planning from the perspective of "How can I help this person get a job now?" rather than "Is this person ready for a job?" Jeremy is an individual who faces several barriers to employment, both disability and non-disability related. Instead of focusing on the problems, this exercise asks you to focus on interests, strengths, and existing capacities in order to move ahead on job development as quickly as possible.

Instructions: Read through the case study below. Spend fifteen minutes answering the questions on the second page as if you are working directly with Jeremy to help him get a job. Identify the strategies identified to help Jeremy get started in looking for a job. Keep in mind the following points:

- Focus on Jeremy's interests and capacities and the resources available, rather then on the problems.
- Don't try to be a psychiatrist, doctor, or social worker and come up with a diagnosis.
- The goal is to get Jeremy a job in his current state of "readiness." Though Jeremy has many issues that need to be addressed in the long term (as many people do), that shouldn't delay the job search. "Fixing" all of one's problems is not a prerequisite to starting a job.

Jeremy

Jeremy is a fifty-year-old man who has lived his entire life at home with his parents in a community near Boston. He has a primary label of cerebral palsy and a secondary label of mental retardation. He also has a history of mental health issues, having been hospitalized numerous times for depressive and psychotic episodes over the years.

Due to his physical disability, Jeremy experiences significant fine motor limitations and uncontrollable drooling. It can be extremely difficult to understand his speech. With age, his strength and endurance capacity seem to be declining. He travels independently on public transportation and is generally known to have lots of energy and be out and about on a daily basis.

Jeremy worked for twenty-five years as a laborer with his local Public Works Department until changes in need and administration caused his "retirement" about three years ago. Since then, periodic medical and dental matters have interrupted his vocational pursuits. His work history also has included brief experiences as groundskeeper at a medical school and mailroom/shipping and receiving clerk at a hospital.

Jeremy has clearly stated his desire to work part-time as a security guard. His interest in this specific arena is quite emphatic, and he is resistant to considering other types of jobs. His father is a former city alderman and worked for years in a state agency, but is hesitant to involve past connections based on bad feelings about previous advocacy efforts.

Jeremy's parents are ambivalent about the job search. They have had little exposure to the human service system, having struggled to provide the best they could for their son on their own. Jeremy has a friend, Jim, whom he met ten years ago at a Bible class. Jim and Jeremy get together regularly to share recreational activities. Jeremy's parents travel extensively, and plan two to three trips per year. It has been assumed that Jeremy will go along because they feel it is unwise to leave him home alone for any length of time. This has greatly impacted the continuity of Jeremy's career search and has limited actual employment options.

Questions about Jeremy

1. What information would you need to gather?

2. Who should be included/consulted in planning? How should they be included?

3. How would you facilitate the planning process to promote Jeremy's being in control and having a respected role?

4. Identify three to five concrete steps you can start within the next few weeks.

2

What Gets
People Jobs?

Many employment agencies serving job seekers with disabilities depend heavily on techniques such as cold calling and responding to classified advertisements for developing job leads. While these methods can and do produce results, research on finding employment for the general population clearly indicates that these strategies are not the most effective use of time and resources. Many of the jobs that are advertised in a major metropolitan newspaper yield hundreds of responses and competition for jobs in local papers can be strong as well.

Job seekers with significant disabilities who get assistance from public and private agencies often are individuals with limited experience and credentials who are weeded out early in the mass response generated by classified ads. Also, research indicates that for job seekers who develop leads through classified advertisements and other cold calls methods, it takes on average ten to twenty cold calls to land one interview, and seven to ten interviews to get a job.

Relying on these methods means it will take seventy to 200 cold calls to get just one job for one job seeker. And, particularly in today's society, most people change jobs and careers many times in their lifetime. The average person will hold eight to ten jobs and have two to three career changes. This could mean 500 to 2,000 cold calls in a lifetime for one person.

These numbers are based on averages – for some people they will be higher and for some lower. Still, multiply these numbers by the number of individuals served by an agency working with people with disabilities. The results are staggering. Clearly, there must be a better way than thumbing through classified ads and cold calling. That better way is using personal connections or "networking."

Using personal connections as a key component of the job search can reduce the number of "no's," improve the odds of getting an interview, and decrease the amount of time a job search can take. It's also generally considered that approximately 60% to 70% of the job market is "hidden," meaning the positions are never advertised. In order for job seekers with disabilities to have a chance at being considered for these positions, the job search needs to include working through personal, community, and organizational connections.

What Is Networking?

Networking refers to a process of informal exchange and created channels to gather information, build support, and get things done. Networks are made up of the connections that we make with people from all walks of life in a variety of settings. The places where people network and the people that we network with are as varied as the diversity of experiences and things that make up day-to-day human existence.

In any place or setting where two people can communicate and exchange information, networking can occur. It happens in any of the settings where we spend time, including home, work, school, and the community.

Examples of people in our network include family, close friends (and not so close friends), former and present employers and co-workers, professionals, school acquaintances and teachers, people with whom we participate in community activities, and people working in stores and businesses we patronize. The size and strength of a network varies, but people all know other people and have networks, probably larger than we realize.

Although networking as a job-seeking strategy has received much attention in recent years, it has been a common business practice for thousands of years, perhaps best expressed in the old adage, "It's not what you know; it's who you know." Business organizations such as the Chamber of Commerce, Rotary Club, and professional organizations are examples of formal networking groups that get together to exchange information for the mutual benefit of all. Over time, membership in these groups transforms formal connections into more personal connections. Other community networks such as religious organizations, health clubs, or recreational interest groups offer opportunities for business people to talk in a less formal manner.

Job development, like sales and marketing, relies on generating new contacts and maintaining relationships with existing customers. Using formal and informal networks is a tried and true method for accomplishing this.

Hiring Research

Research consistently has shown that networking is the most effective job search tool for all job seekers (not just those with disabilities). A 1997 issue of *The Fordyce Letter*, a national business newsletter, included the findings of a survey of a large group of employers.[1] In this survey, employers were asked if they had ever used a variety of methods in their recruitment and hiring practices. The three most prevalent ways that applicants got noticed were by:
- contacting them in person
- responding to a classified advertisement
- being referred by other employees

In fact, the incidence of employee referrals rose 20% from a similar survey conducted two years earlier. The survey also asked employers if they used the Internet in hiring. Twenty-eight percent of employers indicated they had used it, though the satisfaction level was low.

Few employers surveyed had used job fairs or unsolicited resumes for hiring. This information does not mean that you should not use job fairs and unsolicited mailings at all. But, it does send a caution out to individuals who rely only on one or a small number of techniques for finding a job, particularly those techniques that have not been found to be as effective.

The survey results (table above right) emphasize that face-to-face contact, along with employee referrals, are effective. In part this is likely because both methods reduce the "unknown" aspect of the qualifications of the person applying for a position.

Unsolicited walk-ins are used most often (by 96% of businesses) and unsolicited mail-in resumes used the least (1%). This shows that face-to-face contact works! Internet use was mentioned in this survey and it received a 28% rating (mostly larger companies). It is important to note the fact that the job fair rating is low (4%) and that usually it is only the larger employers with human resources departments that can afford to attend job fairs.

THE FORDYCE LETTER
EMPLOYER HIRING
METHODS – 1996

Walk-Ins	96%
Advertising	95%
Employee Ref.	77%
Internet/WWW	28%
State Emp. Serv.	16%
Job Fairs	4%
Direct Mail	1%

Keep in mind that a US government report, *Workforce 2000*, shows that the majority of newly created positions this century will be with small employers, who use job fairs and the Internet less, although use of the Internet is growing quickly.[2] The high use of "walk-ins" and "employee referrals" seems to indicate that employers place value on information that goes beyond paper qualifications.

While the Fordyce survey offers information from the employers perspective, the US Department of Labor (USDOL) has collected data on effective job search practices from the job seekers' perspective.[3] A group of individuals who recently secured employment were asked by USDOL which job search technique yielded their jobs. Sixty-three percent of the respondents got their jobs through informal means such as contacts within the company or information or contacts through family, friends, or neighbors. Only 14% got their jobs through want ads, 12% through private agencies, and 11% through other means such as job fairs, civil service testing, and public agencies.

Both these studies clearly point to the effectiveness of networking as a strategy for obtaining employment.

Since the information cited in these studies pertains to all job seekers, one must assume that the surveys include a percentage of workers with disabilities. A national survey conducted by the Center on Promoting Employment (RRTC) at Children's Hospital, a federally funded grant project at the Institute for Community Inclusion, examined job-search practices specifically for people with disabilities who were receiving services from community rehabilitation agencies.[4] The research looked at people who had recently gotten jobs. It asked what methods the rehabilitation professionals assisting with the job search used to successfully secure employment.

The majority reported that the networking approach was most successful. The most significant findings were that using a networking approach resulted in a higher hourly wage, a greater number of hours worked, and a shorter length of time spent on the job search.

Two other important facts are gleaned from research on employment and people with disabilities.

Fact one:

People with disabilities are more likely to be unemployed than people without disabilities. While the unemployment rate nationwide rarely goes above the single digits, the rate of unemployment for people with disabilities ranges from 60-90%, depending upon the source of the statistic and the definition of disability used. It is clear that economic factors are not the determinant concerning why people with disabilities are unemployed.

Fact two:

People with disabilities have been more likely to rely on professional agencies to secure employment than people without disabilities. However, research on how all people get jobs clearly indicates that it is personal connections that help most people find work. When people with disabilities rely solely on professionals for job placement help and simply "sit back and wait" for the professional to find them a job, they are limiting their opportunities and decreasing their chances of being employed.

Job seekers with disabilities need to use their own networks, as well as those of the placement professionals and organizations that work with them.

DEPARTMENT OF LABOR STATISTICS JOB SEARCH METHODS YIELDING JOBS

Informal	63%
Want Ads	14%
Agencies	12%
Other	11%

Why Networking Is Effective

Literature and training on job hunting for the general population stresses the importance of using one's professional and personal connections to find employment. Yet, in the rehabilitation field, this type of networking is still under-utilized.

Instead, there is overreliance on techniques based on the "numbers game" approach (i.e., make as many contacts as possible, in any way possible, and eventually a job will turn up). While techniques such as searching newspaper classified advertisements, cold calling, filling out applications, and going through the yellow pages do get results, they are time consuming and less successful for job seekers with more significant disabilities.

These individuals, in particular, face significant fear, ignorance, and discrimination in seeking employment. They need the best job-seeking methods available to be able to compete in the job market. The research suggests that not only is networking a successful strategy for assisting any job seeker, but it is an essential element of the job search for job seekers with severe disabilities.

Networking can enable the job seeker to get to the employer "ahead of the pack" before the employer advertises a position, thus cutting down significantly on the competition. This has advantages for both the job seeker and the employer. Many managers use classified ads only as a "last resort" because of the time they have to spend answering calls and screening applicants.

Getting a job (or at least a real shot at being considered for a job) is often a matter of having connections. A job seeker may have terrific skills, but unless an interview with the person who is in a position to hire can be arranged, his or her application or resume will remain one of many lying on the desk.

Networking is based on the assumption that it is human nature to prefer to deal with people one knows and with whom one feels comfortable. Some of the advantages of using your networks are:

- The job developer and job seeker gain credibility through a known relationship.
- Important information regarding who is best to approach, history and needs of the business, and idiosyncrasies of the hiring manager can be obtained.
- The connection can draw attention to an application or resume that may be buried or filed away with dozens or hundreds of others.
- The contact may be able to help avoid initial "screening out" and assist in putting the job developer and applicant directly in contact with the hiring manager.
- It is easier to request support both during the hiring process and after the applicant is hired when there is a connection.

For job seekers with the most significant level of disability, for whom extensive job restructuring and job creation is necessary, using a networking approach is essential. This type of job development method requires extensive involvement and cooperation of both the employer and the employment agency. Developing and strengthening business relationships through personal and professional connections is a very effective strategy in this situation.

Identifying Networks

Usually when individuals are asked to come up with a list of people in their "network," the list is short. One reason is that most people think "Who do I know who can hire?" or "Who is closely connected to someone who can hire?" Remember, your network extends far beyond those people who are in a position to hire directly. It includes everyone you know. Systematically consider all areas of a person's life.

Job developers, other agency staff, administrators, and the board of directors will have a variety of connections that can be a starting point for networking. Job seekers, their families, and friends have community connections that also can be a rich source of potential business connections. Examples of typical personal, organizational, and community connections are listed above right.

PERSONAL CONNECTIONS

Family
Friends
Neighbors
Past employers
Former co-workers

ORGANIZATIONAL CONNECTIONS

Board of directors
Employer advisory board
Contractors and suppliers
Food service, security, banking, teachers and classmates, and grounds keeping services
Other placement professionals

COMMUNITY CONNECTIONS

Church or temple
Chamber of commerce
Clubs and affiliations
Local services, stores, banks

Many people and organizations fail to consider services they use (i.e., places they spend money) as resources. Remember, if an individual or organization is a customer of a company, it is to the company's advantage to strengthen that business relationship by being helpful. Businesses want to keep their customers happy and, as such, can be very helpful resources.

In developing a list of network contacts, write out all the different activities the job seeker is involved in on a daily and weekly basis. Then list the people he or she knows who are involved in those activities. Also, looking back at the person's past life history can help generate networking contacts you may have overlooked (such as past jobs or the college alumnae association).

The list should not be limited to individuals with whom there is a strong connection. Even casual acquaintances can be helpful. However, in developing a contact list, it can be helpful to categorize contacts into stronger and weaker ones.

Approach individuals with whom there is a strong connection first. More can be asked of them, such as assistance in setting up an interview. More casual connections simply may be able to provide additional individuals to contact.

Creating Jobs Through Connections

Using connections is a way of finding out what's going on. It entails connecting with people to gather information and having those people bring others into the process – in essence, using one's network to tap into other people's networks. This gathering of information and meeting new people eventually should lead to meeting the people who are in a position to hire. Through connections, you can find out about current and future job openings, good and bad managers to work for, who is best to talk to in personnel, other people who work in a similar field or business, or which companies/departments are expanding or laying off.

INTRODUCTORY LINES TO NETWORK

"Tell me a little about what you do."

"I'm working with someone who has an interest in working in your field."

"I'm in the process of learning more about jobs in _____ (field).

"Do you know anyone who works in _____?"

"(Contact name) suggested I call you."

"I really value you opinion. I know you can help me in exploring some ideas I have for a person I'm helping to find a job."

"You always seem to have good ideas."

"You seem to know everybody."

"When would be a convenient time to meet?"

"Do you know anyone else I can talk to?"

Not all contacts are going to have specific leads or suggestions. Some will do little to help you, so it is important to be prepared for disappointments. Fear of disappointment should not be a deterrent for taking the initiative to talk to a contact. Each contact could have helpful ideas and suggestions that are worthy of follow-up. In dealing with typical contacts (people not in a position to hire), phrase the request in terms of asking them if they, or anyone they know, works in places that might have the types of jobs the job seeker desires.

NETWORKING: WHAT NOT TO ASK

"Do you know anyone hiring?"
"Are you hiring?"
"Do you know where there are any job openings?"
"Can you get me a job?"

Always ask contacts to provide referrals to other contacts for more information. Also ask permission to use their names as references. If a contact has no leads but seems genuinely interested in helping, it can be worthwhile to keep in touch. A simple thank-you card to all contacts you speak with is recommended as a common courtesy. And let them know how the connections they provided paid off.

Many times a job developer will need to go through several sets of connections to get to the person who is in a position to hire. Eventually, this networking approach will lead to someone related to businesses that might have employment opportunities now or in the future.

Networking is most successful when an individual is able to identify a person in the company who can influence the hiring process. This advocate or "champion" doesn't have to be a "head honcho"– only someone with the belief in the cause of hiring people with disabilities and some connections to draw upon.

Champions often are people who for a variety of reasons have more than just a professional interest. Maybe someone once gave them a chance or they have a family member who has a disability. After identifying champions, give them free rein and lots of support, appreciation, and recognition for their efforts.

Making, expanding, and using contacts to develop jobs requires that a job developer makes it part of his or her everyday routine to talk to people on line at the grocery store, to neighbors walking home, and to others waiting in the dentist's office. It entails asking all the people you meet what they do for a living.

This is not intrusive. People like to talk about themselves and what they do. Job seekers and those helping them never know when they will meet someone who is in a position to offer assistance or information.

Successful job developers make networking a part of their everyday life. Creating jobs through networks extends beyond the job developers to others connected with the agency. Job seekers, their family members, agency staff, administration, and the board of directors can and should be trained, supported, and expected to use their connections to assist in developing job opportunities.

Why People Don't Network

A networking approach is effective, but it is not easy for everyone. Many people don't like or feel comfortable with initiating contact and the social interactions that are part of networking. While job developers, job seekers, and agency staff may understand the importance of this approach, they may have trouble putting it into practice.

In day-to-day interactions, total strangers talk to one another. For example, people stop strangers on the street to ask the time or for directions. These requests usually are met with helpful information. Very rarely will total strangers not answer requests for help.

If this is true of strangers, imagine what it is like when there is a connection between the people. In general, most people feel good about being asked for help. In many ways being asked for help is a compliment and an indication of respect. So what keeps people from asking the people they know for help?

Some of the common reasons people feel uncomfortable networking are: they're scared, they don't feel comfortable asking for help or don't want to feel like they owe someone for helping, they don't believe they (or the people they represent) are worthy of help from others, or they worry about the impact it will have on their relationship with the person they asked for help.

When you start thinking this way, remember the research. Most job seekers use networking to get jobs and most employers view it as a preferred method of hiring employees. Businesses all over the world employ it daily to get and keep customers. Successful job developers practice and perfect this technique.

The more the job developer and job seeker use this technique, the more comfortable they will get. Generally speaking, the outcome will be positive, and certainly better than one's worst fears – and people are often flattered by the call. If a reasonable request for assistance is made, most people try to help. If this still seems like a daunting and uncomfortable task, try one or more of the following:

- If some support would help, bring someone.
- A familiar face may be a comfortable way to begin.
- Start with someone with whom there is less to lose.
- Some settings are easier than others. Try talking with someone while participating in an activity together, such as softball practice, at the health club, or during a social gathering.
- Try to meet in person. This will encourage a longer conversation.

WHY PEOPLE DON'T NETWORK

FEAR:
People tend to be afraid of the unknown. Until one uses networks, it can be scary.

PRIDE:
Many individuals are too proud to ask for assistance.

DEPENDENCY:
There is a feeling that asking for assistance in a job search makes one seem dependent. Networking is the recommended approach to job searches. This is not dependency.

DOUBT:
Many people worry that they are not worthy of help, and that people will say "no."

EMBARRASSMENT:
For some, being in a position of need is uncomfortable and embarrassing.

Broadening Connections

When existing personal and professional connections are not enough to find jobs for all job seekers in the organization, expand the network of connections. Though this takes time and effort, it pays off in the long run in expanding employment opportunities. Some ideas for expanding networks are:

- Develop secondary networks: ask current personal and professional contacts for other contacts.
- Develop an employer advisory board/business advisory council.
- Have staff join business and community groups on company time.

22

- Get involved in local politics, local planning boards, and economic redevelopment advisory groups.
- Have current business contacts facilitate introductions to other department heads and managers.
- Market the agency to the business community as disability consultants.
- Ask a local employer or group (such as the Rotary Club) to sponsor an agency program.

One thing that will make the efforts more productive is to focus on trying to meet people who have lots of connections themselves and who are good at helping other people make connections. That's why you ask contacts if they know anyone who might be helpful as well.

These resources can be a gold mine that not only helps in finding a job now, but in the future as well. The connections that help most people get jobs are not the people in the job developer's or job seeker's close circle (parents, relatives, close friends). Rather, they are the casual contacts such as neighbors, former co-workers, and connections you make through the people closest to you. This requires continual work at expanding networks.

Exercise 2-A
Brainstorming Contacts

Purpose: To better understand the value of a group brainstorming process for generating contacts.

Instructions: John is a consumer you are assisting in finding a job. After extensive planning and career exploration, he has indicated that his dream job would be working at a funeral parlor. Develop a list of people and places to contact that could help lead to a job at a funeral parlor for John.

People to contact:

Places to research:

Exercise 2-B
Identifying Personal Networks

Purpose: To practice identifying networks of other individuals.

Instructions: Obtain two index cards. Write your name on each one. On one card write a topic with which you are very familiar; and on the other card write a topic about which you want to learn. Post these cards on a wall. The goal is to network in order to find out more about your topic of interest, as well as to share information relating to other people's needs. Go in with an open mind, because sometimes the conversation will not go as planned. Be flexible and willing to be steered in different directions. These new paths may end up being helpful. Try to connect with at least two people.

How did you do with networking?

Did you get what you wanted to learn?

How did it feel to ask for information?

How did it feel to share information with others?

Did any new information come your way?

How can this apply to job development?

3

When There Is No Connection

When networking is difficult because of a lack of connections to the business community, a good place to start your marketing is to develop your understanding of the local labor market. Local labor market information is available from a number of sources including Department of Labor publications, the Chamber of Commerce, the Internet, and local employers or business groups.

Knowledge about the local labor market is an important tool for any job developer. It provides developers with current data about:

- the type, size, and location of particular businesses and industries
- the types of jobs, skill, and educational requirements
- projections about which businesses or industries will be expanding
- where new and different types of employment opportunities will be created

A market survey is one strategy for getting very targeted information. Conducting a market survey involves contacting a selected group of businesses from a particular industry or in a particular location and asking them a group of questions. The questions are designed to gain information about job opportunities now and in the future, business demands, expectations, and workplace culture, and to identify key contacts within the company.

LOCAL LABOR MARKET ANALYSIS

1. Who are the major employers in your area?
2. What types of employment are found most?
3. Which companies/types of employment have the highest turnover?
4. Which companies/types of employment are anticipating growth soon?
5. Which companies are known to hire people with disabilities?
6. Where does your community have seasonal employment?

This strategy is a very effective tool for quickly learning more about a segment of the local labor market and identifying job opportunities in industries with which you are unfamiliar. This survey approach is also an easy and effective way to make initial contacts with employers that you don't know, thus minimizing the chance of rejection.

MARKETING SURVEY

1. Target employer market.
2. Introduce survey.
3. Conduct survey.
4. Distribute results.
5. Contact selected employers.

A sample marketing survey is included at the end of this section and at left to illustrate the type of questions you might ask an employer. Consider factors such as size, type of business, and business structure (e.g., franchise versus locally owned store) when figuring out who to contact. A marketing survey can be used with one industry (e.g., eight to ten hotels in your area) or within a particular locale (e.g., all stores within a mall or businesses in an industrial park).

Below are some considerations in developing and implementing a market survey.

1) It is best to ask the questions in person, or at a minimum over the phone. Avoid sending out a survey to be filled out and returned by mail.

2) For a very large business, first try contacting the CEO, vice president, or operations manager. If you have to settle for working through human resources, speak with the HR manager. In a small business, ask to speak to the owner. Before contacting the business, check to see if they have a website, which can help you gain information about the company and personnel.

3) State departments of employment and training or One-Stop Career Centers can give detailed information about industries across the state, within counties, and within a particular town or city. Records at city halls can provide information on business licensees, tax records, and other data available to the public. The Chamber of Commerce can provide member lists. Private entities such as human resource associations, health care groups, and farming organizations also may be willing to provide information. Much of this is now available through the Internet.

4) Have an organization like a Chamber of Commerce sponsor the marketing survey. This gives it higher visibility and credibility, makes contacting the individual businesses easier, and aids in follow-up steps.

5) Follow-up on surveys should be done through personalized thank-you letters or cards. These little niceties can make a lasting impression.

A caution regarding using labor market information is that job development needs to be driven by the interests, skills, and preferences of the job seekers the agency serves. A survey provides valuable information to use in developing job opportunities for individual applicants based on their career plans. The information gathered through a local labor market survey or other marketing survey assists with career exploration and identifying potential job opportunities in industries or particular businesses unfamiliar to job developers. However, a job seeker with a disability, like any one else does, wants a job that is a good match with interests, skills, and working conditions, which may be different from what jobs are most available in the region.

A market survey of a section of Cape Cod in Massachusetts will indicate that there are many restaurant and motel job opportunities in the summer. Investing time in developing relationships with these employers makes sense only if the job developer has, or will have, job seekers with interests and skills in these areas.

While the skills, background, experiences, interests, and dreams of the job seeker should be the basis of deciding what businesses to approach for job development, do not be strictly limited by these. Bear in mind that everyone is the sum of their experiences. People with disabilities, who may have had limited work and life experiences, can have a limited frame of reference about job and career possibilities.

Job developers, like anyone, also can be limited by their experiences. The job developer's expertise on the wide variety of jobs and professions that exist in a region can be fairly limited, more so than the person may realize. One reason so many people with disabilities are placed in retail and food service jobs is because that is "what we know" – everyone shops and eats.

It is important for both the job seeker and job developer to bear in mind that there is a wide variety of businesses, jobs, and careers in the world of work. It's important to "peek behind" some of the closed doors of businesses, to find out what they do and what types of job possibilities may exist.

Using the personal, professional, and community connections of job seekers, staff, and the agency is clearly the easiest and most effective way to make initial contacts with employers. However, job developers will not always have connections to every business they may want to contact. There are other effective methods for getting one's foot in the door.

Job seekers with and without disabilities get jobs all the time through classified advertisements in newspapers, walking in and filling out an application, and making cold calls using the Yellow Pages. The key is having an understanding of which strategies will be most effective with individual job seekers, employers, and types of jobs.

There are also ways to gather information about a particular business without direct contact with a representative from that company. These methods can be used alone as an initial step or in conjunction with a market survey or other approach. They are listed in the table that follows.

Variables such as the skills, experience, and presentation of the job seeker in relation to other applicants need to be considered. Also consider the likelihood of an employer's screening out a job applicant who stopped by to fill out an application or called in response to a classified advertisement.

The size and nature of a business are important in deciding what type of approach to use and whom to contact initially in the company (i.e., telephone call, dropping in). While it may be most natural and expedient to drop in at the local hardware store and ask to speak to the owner, an initial cold contact to a large insurance company more likely should be done with a phone call to personnel. Likewise, the type of job (accountant versus dishwasher) is another consideration in terms of approach.

While you might drop by both an accounting firm and a local restaurant, the approach will be different. With the former, you might walk in and ask to leave a resume while setting up an appointment with personnel or the manager, depending on the size of the company. With the restaurant, you would be more likely to ask to speak to the manager or owner right away. Though each circumstance will be different, the good job developer needs to be able to read the situation and act accordingly.

In-person cold calling can be a useful strategy where job development efforts must focus on a specific geographic area. It can yield unexpected dividends in discovering businesses the job developer was previously unaware of. Some job developers also have successfully used in-person cold calling as an information gathering approach, casually getting information on types of possible jobs available, hiring practices, and the contact person for hiring. Armed with this specific information, the job developer then calls the business on the phone, uses the contact name, and cites specific information in the interaction.

Mass mailing as the initial contact is time consuming and expensive, and not worth the resources required. Mailings targeted to specific employers can be more effective. In a direct mail approach, a follow-up phone call will increase the response rate. It is the extremely rare employer that will take the initiative and call a job developer or agency they don't know as the result of a letter. The possible exception is in a very tight labor market.

One effective use of direct mail is sending a letter to employers under the signature and letterhead of a prominent individual (politician, celebrity, community leader, or major employer). This works particularly well if such letters are targeted towards employers the prominent individual knows personally. But again, without a follow-up phone call, such an approach is not likely to produce results.

After considering and deciding upon which methods to use in making initial contacts with employers, getting started with each individual job seeker requires some initial planning. Job development is most effective when there is a written plan that delineates:
- employers to call/visit
- other contacts to pursue
- actions to be taken by the applicant, job developer, or others
- timelines for when these actions will occur

Review and revise these plans every thirty days until the person is successfully employed. Although no one is a fan of additional paperwork, this simple process effectively keeps the job search process on track and increases accountability of all parties.

Knowing the local labor market helps you identify what opportunities exist and which businesses to target. Easily available resources to gather information include: Department of Labor publications, the Chamber of Commerce, the Internet, and local employers or business groups. The process of contacting individual employers or business groups also serves as an easy way to get a foot in the door with local employers in the community.

SAMPLE LABOR MARKET SURVEY

1. Who are the major employers in your area?

2. What types of employment are found most?

3. Which companies/types of employment have the highest turnover?

4. Which companies/types of employment are anticipating growth soon?

5. Which companies are known to hire people with disabilities?

6. Where does your community have seasonal employment?

Exercise 3-A
Market Survey

Purpose: To design a market survey and develop strategies for implementing this approach including: 1) which businesses to target, 2) whom to target within the company, 3) how to present the survey, 4) next steps after initial contact is made.

Instructions: Identify a particular industry that you have either not approached or not been successful in developing employment opportunities with.

How would you decide which businesses to target?

Who would you contact within the companies?

How would you introduce yourself and the survey?

Are there any other questions you would ask in addition to those on the sample survey?

What next steps would you take after completing the survey?

Exercise 3-B
Evaluating the
Effectiveness of Approaches

Purpose: To identify the variety of ways to contact employers when there is no personal or professional connection, and to think through which strategies are most and least effective for which job seekers, which industries, and which types of jobs.

Instructions: Write down ways to approach businesses when you or your agency has no prior personal or professional connection. Then, consider with which types of job seekers, types of companies (nature of business; size; rural, suburban, or urban location), and types of jobs each approach listed would work most effectively and least effectively. As you do this, think of specific individuals or companies with whom you are working.

Approaches	Job Seekers	Types of Companies	Types of Jobs
1.			
2.			
3.			
4.			
5.			
6.			

Exercise 3-C
Developing a Thirty-Day Placement Plan

Purpose: To combine a variety of methods in initiating job development activities using a thirty-day placement plan format.

Instructions: Focus on a job seeker you work with who is in the initial stages of job development. The profile should include job goal(s), age, skills, work experiences, job seeking skills and limitations, other interests, hobbies or activities, family and other personal/community contacts, and other pertinent information relevant to the job hunt. Using the Thirty-Day Placement Plan form below, identify a minimum of six steps to take in the next thirty days to contact employers, using at least three of the techniques that have been covered in this training (including networking). When developing these steps, consider the effectiveness of different approaches in making employer contacts.

THIRTY-DAY PLACEMENT PLAN

Job Seeker: **Date:**

Job Goal:

The job seeker has the following skills, experience, and personal qualities for this job:

These individuals have committed to do the following to achieve this goal:

When will this be reviewed again?

Signatures of:

Job Seeker: Staff:

Other(s) who have offered to help:

Exercise 3-D
Developing a Marketing Strategy

Purpose: To further develop abilities to develop contacts with employers.

Instructions: You are currently assisting a woman who is interested in working in the health care industry. Never Get Sick Health Plan (NGSHP) has recently opened a new large health center in your community and has been running want ads in the newspaper for a variety of positions including clerical, laboratory, housekeeping, and medical/clinical. The person has limited job experience and you are fearful that if she submits a job application through the human resources department, she will be screened out. Use the questions below as a guide to assist you in approaching NGSHP to open employment opportunities for this individual (and possibly others) served by your agency.

1. What types of personal, organizational, and community connections could you use to make initial contact with NGSHP?

2. Who will you contact at NGSHP?

3. How could you gather more information about NGSHP and employment opportunities prior to meeting with NGSHP?

   - Go to business library (KIRSTEN)
   - "   "   uMass Amherst
   - follow up thank you note

4. What are some strategies that you will use in developing a relationship with NGSHP beyond the first contact?

4

Getting Past the Front Door

Now is the time to get beyond the theory and use the information you have learned to develop your personal style of job development. It is the time to go out and "just do it." What stops us? We all have heard the following lament, or a variation of it, time and time again. "I know all about social skills, and I have attended placement training. I just don't feel comfortable going out and doing it." But job development, by definition, involves doing it.

Every individual has the capacity to make contacts, though the style and ease of making contacts varies. Some people meet others while waiting on line in a grocery store, at a deli counter, or on the train. Some people may be more reserved in their approach and require more time and structure to connect with people. They may need to join a social group or become involved in a community activity, then after time begin to develop contacts there. Whatever the method, developing contacts involves talking to people with whom one does not have an existing relationship.

Meeting and interacting with new people is influenced by first impressions. And in the job development business, making the most positive first impression is critical.

While every person likes to think of him or herself as fitting in well and getting along with others, sometimes people are unaware of how they come across. The nicest, most outgoing person may come across as slick to some. An introverted individual may appear to be standoffish or a snob.

The successful job developer is aware of what impression he or she makes on others and uses this information to shape a presentation style and content. For example, the slick-appearing extrovert may wish to mention personal interests or activities that

indicate more depth. The introvert may work into a discussion activities that reflect the fact that the individual values people. Whatever the technique, you can use the information gained about first impressions to develop a personal marketing style and presentation that works.

Job Development as a Lifestyle

The next part of making contacts involves a certain amount of small talk or "schmoozing." This too is based on personality and interests. Some individuals are good at talking about everything and anything. Other people need to find personal connections or interests in common.

However you do it, you need to become at ease with people and work to find your own style. The myth that one must be a smooth-talking sales person or extremely outgoing is inaccurate. Job developers come in all shapes and sizes. They range in personality. The only prerequisites for this work are that you believe that people with disabilities can and should work and that they can make a valuable contribution to the workplace. Beyond that, you need only find a style that is comfortable and effective for outreach to employers. Develop an ability to read employers' reactions and modify the approach as needed.

As a general rule, job development is a lifestyle rather than a nine-to-five job. Remember that networking and making contacts can happen at any time and any place. For example, social gatherings provide wonderful opportunities to talk with new people about what they do and to learn more about them. Weddings, holiday parties, open houses, religious gatherings, sporting activities, social groups, and service group gatherings all provide opportunities to talk with many people. While interacting with people in these and other settings, keep an ear open for potential job development contacts.

You can talk about work and hand out business cards. Reminding people about information and expertise that the job developer is willing to share helps to warm up connections. These interactions occasionally will yield leads. Sometimes they may develop into discussions of family members with disabilities. Or the exchange may go nowhere beyond a pleasant conversation.

Handling Gatekeepers

For the more formal work of job development, there are differing styles for phone and in-person interactions with employers or their gatekeepers. Most businesses have screening mechanisms that keep callers from talking to the "big boss."

These gatekeepers, often receptionists or administrative assistants, perfect their telephone manner and usually successfully prevent what they perceive as unwanted calls from trickling past them to their managers. They could provide helpful information, such as when the manager is more available, but they are unlikely to volunteer such information.

Thus, talking with the gatekeeper is an art. Finding ways to interact that continue the conversation rather than terminate it is a skill that is devel-

oped over time. An experienced job developer learns to be friendly but persistent. There are tricks to getting through, such as:

- name dropping if there is a contact
- offering to call back at a more convenient time
- offering to wait for the person to get off the phone
- asking a technical question that the gatekeeper cannot answer

Getting the gatekeeper's name and being friendly over the phone may help, though seasoned gatekeepers quickly can see through a lack of sincerity. For example, an effective approach might be, "Hi Joan, it's Susan calling again for John Carlton. How are you doing? Is he available? I know he's busy. Could you suggest what would be a less hectic time for me to catch him?"

This kind of interaction lets Joan see that you are reasonably nice and value her advice. Some job developers find that early morning or late afternoon hours are good for finding the manager with no gatekeeper on duty. You can use these approaches both in person and over the phone. Whatever the method, there is no one surefire way to get past the gatekeeper. The successful job developer has a bag of tricks ready and uses them assertively and with persistence.

Eight Tips for Telephone Contacts

1. Improve Your Timing.
   Schedule your calls when you know your target will be in. Early morning, midweek, and mid-month are good times. Calls made on Monday mornings, Friday afternoons, and at the end of the month are likely to fail.

2. Have an Alternative Contact.
   Develop a second or third contact within a company who can handle your call if your first choice is unavailable.

3. **Know the Secretaries.**
   The secretary often screens, fields, and prioritizes calls. Make friends with this person.

4. **Know When to Hold 'em; Know When to Fold 'em.**
   You waste precious minutes on hold that could be productive. When your call is finally put through, the target may be unprepared and not in the mood for another call.

5. **Leave Clever Messages.**
   Define the desired action and time frame. Pique the target's interest or use a little light humor - but don't overdo it.

6. **Make Use of High-Tech Systems.**
   Don't let voice mail, answering machines, electronic mailboxes, or call processing put you off. These devices are for your convenience – learn to use them to your advantage.

7. **Get the Important Information.**
   Find out when the person will return, if he or she is expected to be busy then, and when the best time is to attempt another call.

8. **Know When to Quit.**
   Stop calling when all methods have been exhausted.

Personal Contact

The next step is knowing what to say when you finally reach the employer. Whether the initial communication is by phone or an unscheduled in-person visit, remember the goal at this point is *not* to get a job. It is simply to get an appointment, either immediately or later on, to gather and exchange information and further the relationship. Think of the analogy of dating or a courtship. Just as an individual doesn't ask someone to marry them the first time they meet, developing a working relationship with an employer to the point where a job can be developed takes time.

Aim for face-to-face contact. Polite reminders, while you are accessible and cooperative, leave a pleasant aftertaste to interactions. If you call to confirm and the person must cancel, be positive about rescheduling. This may tap into the person's sense of guilt for having to cancel, and the actual meeting may go better. Stress the desire to get ideas, information, suggestions, and other contacts from each employer. Also, look to keep the doors open

for future interactions, such as checking in and keeping him or her posted.

An information-gathering approach often is best used on the first contact with an employer. Suggested opening lines might include:

"I work for a nonprofit organization that helps people who are out of work find jobs. We have successfully placed people in _____ (businesses with successful placements, particularly those in the same field as the business being contacted). What would be a good time to meet so I can learn about your business needs and share some information about the program and the people I represent?"

"I'm working with someone who is interested in this business, and I would like to learn more about it."

"I work for a nonprofit organization that helps people find jobs. We're currently canvassing the business community to get a better handle on employer needs."

These are just suggestions. Each job developer will want to come up with others that suit his or her style and comfort level. Bear in mind, though, that your goal at this point is simply to move the relationship forward, not to get a job. Whatever the words and approach you use, practice your initial "pitch" until you have it "down cold." You must be totally comfortable in this initial interaction, and come across with sincerity and confidence.

Is it a good idea to use the word disability in an opening line? Clearly, if you are representing individuals who have indicated that they do not want the fact that they have a disability disclosed to potential employers, then you should not use the word "disability." However, in cases where the disability is not "hidden," where in the process of developing a relationship with an employer should you mention this? Or should the job developer wait until the employer meets the individual?

This is dependent chiefly on the job seekers preferences. Job developers often have concerns about mentioning that they work with people with disabilities, because of the potential negative reaction from employers. In a case where some level of disclosure is going to occur, job developers should be prepared to explain what disability really means in an effort to overcome the myths, misconceptions, and stereotypes often held about people with disabilities.

INTERACTING WITH CONTACTS

- Use the person's name.
- Ask "Is this a good time?"
- Offer to send a resume.
- Meet at the contact's convenience.
- Ask the contact to pass the resume to others.
- Confirm the meeting one day before.
- Don't ask for a job.
- Ask to keep in touch.

The job developer also needs to be prepared to react appropriately to whatever the situation presents. For example, you may walk into a business hoping to secure an appointment at some point in the future. However, the employer may be available to meet immediately and have a need to hire someone right away. Or, the employer may be resistant to setting up a meeting or start asking the job developer questions about the agency's services.

An ability to effectively handle such interactions is truly both a skill and an art. It takes time and practice to become proficient. For example, when an employer starts asking lots of questions, you can defer him or her by saying, "Rather than spend lots of time answering questions now when you're busy, why don't we set up a convenient time to meet where we can talk more at length?" If an employer is resistant to meeting, probing at the underlying reasons behind his or her resistance can be helpful. The job developer also should emphasize the low level of commitment being asked for: "I would like to meet just for a few minutes. I just want to bounce some ideas off you as a successful business person."

Style of Interacting

There are different communication styles, and there is no one perfect style. You need to find your most effective approach. Sincerity, honesty, and a belief in what you are doing - no matter what your style - will work. Looking for ways to connect with a person, such as observing a picture on the desk or plaques on wall may provide an entry into chat that reduces the tension or formality of the interaction. This must be done in a manner mutually comfortable for the employer and the job developer. It is important not to cross boundaries by assuming a familiarity that is not yet established. Styles will vary from job developer to job developer. They should be modified to match the relationship with each employer.

SOME DIFFERENT STYLES

- forceful
- laid back
- informational and problem solving
- "slick" sales
- soft sell
- hard sell

When following up with contacts, personalize the interactions. For example, if you meet and learn the individual is about to embark on a week-long hiking vacation, you could include a question about the vacation in the follow-up interaction. Making notes about people's specific details in a Rolodex or job development log helps to personalize future contacts.

Different styles match different situations. Adjust your style as necessary. It is helpful to receive feedback on style. Remember that image and dress are important to set the tone for the interaction.

SOME BASIC RULES FOR STYLE

- Fit your style to the person you are interacting with:
  - strictly business
  - social and gregarious
  - eccentric

- Exhibit sincerity in your interactions and belief in what and who you are marketing.

- Look for a personal connection.

- Get a "read" on the situation and react appropriately.

Exercise 4-A
First Impressions

Purpose: To evaluate the first impressions you make on others and how this can affect employer interactions.

Instructions: Pair up with someone whom you don't know well. Each person should have two copies of the First Impressions form on the next page. Take a few minutes and check off five items on the list that best reflect you. Check a minimum of three items and a maximum of ten. Then, take the second sheet, record the name of the other person on top, and rate the other person for the first impressions made. When both of you have completed this task, share the ratings of one another and compare the self-rating with the other observer's rating.

What surprises did you find when comparing sheets?

Were people accurate in their ratings? Why or why not?

Were any opposite terms selected? Which ones?

How can this information help us?

Do you consider some terms to be negative? Which ones?

How might they be negative in some settings and not in others?

Did you learn anything about yourself?

First Impressions

_____ Thoughtful	_____ Funny	_____ Responsible
_____ Calm	_____ Happy	_____ Outgoing
_____ Impulsive	_____ Friendly	_____ Professional
_____ Hard-Working	_____ Motivated	_____ Laid Back
_____ Modest	_____ Honest	_____ Quick to Answer
_____ Disorganized	_____ Polite	_____ Organized
_____ Mature	_____ Serious	_____ Conservative
_____ Impatient	_____ Nervous	_____ Angry
_____ Shy	_____ Reserved	_____ Ambitious
_____ Casual	_____ Lazy	_____ Smooth Talking
_____ Energetic	_____ Confident	_____ Immature
_____ Patient	_____ Silly	_____ Formal

Which words best describe you?
What do others think?

Exercise 4-B
Getting Beyond the Gatekeeper

Purpose: To practice telephone interactions in dealing with the "gatekeeper" or secretary.

Instructions: Role play with another individual. One person is an obstructionist secretary. The other is the job developer. The job developer must role play a telephone interaction with the secretary, with the goal of speaking directly with the hiring manager. The person playing the secretary should not make this an easily attained goal. The role-play should be kept to under two minutes.

Whom did you choose to role play with and why?

What struck you as effective techniques to reach the hiring manager?

What did you like about the role play?

What didn't you like?

What other strategies might be used that weren't?

Exercise 4-C
Role Play: Face-to-Face with an Employer

Purpose: To practice and evaluate what makes an effective interaction with employers.

Instructions: This exercise is done by two individuals. In the role-play, one person is the employer (a person in a hiring capacity) and the other person is the job developer. The job developer has walked into the business without an appointment and asked the receptionist for the manager. The manager has come out to the reception area, and the job developer introduces him or herself. The job developer's goal is to make this as positive an interaction as possible, which will lead to identification of possible employment opportunities. The job developer has not had previous contact with this business.

1. What did you think about this employer?

2. Have you had any interactions like this one?

3. What actions of the job developer did you like?

4. What did you not feel comfortable with?

5. What might you do differently?

6. How would you follow up on this meeting?

7. Is walking in on an employer without an appointment like this a good approach?

8. In what situations would this approach be appropriate?

9. In what situations would this approach be inappropriate?

5

Effective Marketing Strategies

This section confronts the dilemma often heard from beginning job developers: "I went into this field to help others, not to become a salesperson." Marketing is relevant to job development. Marketing a product is very similar to the work a job developer must do to succeed. You must know the product (in this case a potential employee and your services), highlight assets, and downplay liabilities, and do so with confidence in a creative and positive manner.

The first component of marketing is dealing effectively with people. As discussed in the previous section, most everyone has basic social skills. Working on refining them increases one's effectiveness in job development.

Marketing also involves selling, which is simply meeting a need or selling to an area of interest. To do this, you first must find out what the potential buyer's needs and interests are and then present a product in a way that fills those needs. Finally, you must know the product well enough to identify both its assets and liabilities. A successful marketing strategy involves promoting the product (the job seeker) by highlighting the assets and neutralizing or downplaying the liabilities.

Finding Opportunities

As noted in earlier sections, a base of information about the job seeker is generated through good planning and assessment. Then you can use this information to explore employment options. Identifying employment opportunities requires that the job developer determine what business need can be met by hiring a person with a disability. Three categories of benefits to employers of hiring people with disabilities were identified during focus group discussion with employers recently conducted by the Institute for Community Inclusion in collaboration with the Center for Work and Family at Boston College.[5] These were:

- **Benefits of Hiring Directly Related to Business Objectives**
  Hiring people with disabilities will meet the personnel needs of the organization by filling vacant positions.

- **Benefits Indirectly Related to Business Objectives**
  A decision to hire individuals with disabilities will benefit a company's viability or profitability in a way that is indirectly related to short-term business objectives, by enhancing the corporate image and demonstrating a commitment to the community.

- **Benefits Related to Organizational Values**
  A decision to hire people with disabilities is based on fulfilling the values of an organization, such as a commitment to diversifying the work force, being a socially responsible business, or hiring people with disabilities as "the right thing to do" as a member of the business community.

Often a combination of these factors is behind the decision to hire a person with a disability. However, even if the benefit to the employer is not directly related to business objectives, none of these potential benefits should be misconstrued merely as an act of charity. It is still paramount for the long-term success of the individual, and of people with disabilities in general, that the job be performed competently in a socially inclusive work environment.

The main difference is that if the employer views the benefits of hiring a person with a disability as needing to directly relate to business objectives, then the responsibility rests on the job developer and the job seeker to prove to the employer that hiring the individual provides direct economic benefit. There also probably will be less flexibility around how the job is designed and the individual is supported.

On the other hand, if the benefits are viewed as indirectly related to business objectives or related to organizational values, you have an opportunity for greater flexibility or more creative solutions - the employer views hiring a person with a disability beyond the direct economic benefit that it provides to the business, and the business is committed to "making it work."

Experience has shown that a number of employers have initially hired a person with a disability for reasons other than those directly related to business objectives, but later have admitted that they were "pleasantly surprised" that the person turned out to be a "good employee." What these types of experiences make clear is that there is much to be done to change the general public's perception of people with disabilities as competent citizens. Also indicated is that the benefits to an employer in hiring a new employee must be looked at more broadly than just economically.

Prior to meeting with an employer, the job developer may be able to identify potential employer needs through research and network contacts. If an employer is very active in the community, views community relations as important, or has expressed the need for businesses to be socially responsible and to "give back" to their communities, the "pitch" of the job developer should reflect these identified needs.

While identifying these types of needs potentially could make the "sell" easier, it is still important to emphasize why a particular individual is a good match for the specific needs of an employer. On the other hand, if an employer recently has experienced an economic downturn or is a new business, a small business with a thin bottom line, or simply a business with a reputation for being strictly focused on economic benefit, the job developer should use an approach that focuses on these needs.

Needs also may vary within businesses. For instance, the owner or manager of a business or the human resource department may view hiring a person with a disability as important in the efforts to diversify the work force. But this may not have been adequately communicated to the operations manager of the department where the person will be working, nor be his or her priority. This was noted by the previously cited focus groups conducted by the Center for Work and Family at Boston College.

In essence, the view of the manager or frontline supervisor may be something akin to "Diversity sounds great, but I've got operational goals and a budget I still have to meet." Therefore, the job developer should meet with the operations manager and make every effort to gain an understanding of the needs within the actual department where the person will be working. By doing so, the job developer can determine whether the needs of the particular department are different from other parts of the organization (such as human resources) and, if so, how to respond to them.

The job developer and job seeker should use a systematic approach in gathering information from employers to identify potential employment opportunities. While this does not necessarily mean that the job developer should have a twelve-page checklist when visiting an employer, he or she should meet an employer with the intention of gathering specific information that is needed to develop jobs and ensure a good job match.

New job developers in particular should have a written outline of information that they need to gather, so that in the sometimes pressured and tension-filled atmosphere of meeting with an employer, they don't forget to ask or observe certain things. For example, the job developer or job seeker may focus so much on the specifics of what a business does that he or she fails to note the social culture of the workplace.

During initial discussions with an employer, the job developer must ask questions and gain information to determine what the employer needs are. Questions concerning business objectives and challenges, their perception of what constitutes a "good employee," and past experience with people with disabilities will help provide the necessary information.

Part of the information gathering also must focus on the workplace culture and support available. Through questions and observation, the job developer and job seeker should consider such issues as how formal or informal the workplace is, the level of socializing that occurs both on and off the job, how supportive employees are of each other, the level of independence that is expected, the flexibility of duties and roles, adherence to rules and regulations, unwritten "rules" of the workplace, social rituals that occur, and the type of people who already work there.

You also should note the amount of training and level of supervision that typically is offered. This can help evaluate whether the business is a place where the job seeker will fit in and be comfortable, and whether it can provide the support the individual requires. If it seems to be a good match, this information is used by the job developer and job seeker to tailor their approach to the needs and preferences of that particular employer.

Title I of the ADA states that an individual with a disability must be able to perform the "essential functions" of a job. Therefore, part of the job developers' and job seekers' responsibility in the information-gathering portion of job development is to get a handle on the essential requirements of the job. It will help if you can obtain a written job description from the employer.

The essential functions of the job are important to know from both a legal and practical sense. This helps you determine whether or not the job is a good match for the job seeker, provide a basis for negotiating and advocating with the employer, and if necessary, decide if discriminatory practices are taking place. If disclosure of the disability has taken place, you can focus specifically on the essential functions of the job and how the person with a disability is able to perform those functions (with or without reasonable accommodation). You may have to make gentle reminders about the job seekers rights under the ADA, but only if circumstances warrant it.

Also bear in mind that the job seeker's personality often can be the deciding factor in the hiring decision, beyond meeting a business need. (This is true for people with and without disabilities.) If an employer likes the job seeker, barriers posed by typical stereotypes of people with disabilities can break down, and the employer may be more willing to identify or create an opportunity for the individual and provide the necessary supports. For example, an employer initially may be hesitant about hiring someone with a disability, but after meeting the job seeker may get past the disability stereotype and find the person to be interesting, funny, good company, or demonstrating a good work ethic. In turn, the employer will make the effort to identify a position for the person.

There are many people who aren't particularly likable, yet who are successfully employed. (Everyone knows at least one.) As with other challenges, good job matching is key to successful employment of individuals with personalities that may be perceived as "difficult." It helps to remember that what may be perceived as a negative personality in one setting may be viewed differently in another. For example, verbally aggressive people can be annoying, but they can be viewed as assets in jobs requiring aggressive approaches such as payment collections. These individuals also may work successfully in jobs where there is limited interaction with others, such as night security or stock work.

DISABILITY LABEL AND MARKETING

- Does the person want to be represented to the employer by a professional?
- Does the person wish to disclose to the employer?
- What are the implications of disclosing/not disclosing?
- Is disability "hidden" or readily apparent to potential employers?

Disclosure

The topic of disclosure is frequently a difficult one for job developers. The following are among the questions most frequently asked by job development personnel.

JOB DEVELOPER QUESTIONS ON DISCLOSURE

- How should disclosure be handled?
- How much information are we supposed to share?
- Aren't we lying if we don't disclose?
- What about the relationship with the employer and the business community?
- Does not disclosing taint the relationship with the employer?
- Won't this discredit our agency?

Hidden Disabilities

When dealing with a "hidden disability" (i.e., a disability that is not readily apparent to most people), there is the option of not disclosing. The decision about disclosure is a personal one to be made by the individual with a disability. The role of the job developer is to assist the job seeker in thinking through the consequences of disclosing/nondisclosing, to support the person's decision, and to devise a job development plan based on that decision. Such a complicated decision requires consideration of items below.

- **Personal ethics of the job seeker?**
  How does the person view the issue of nondisclosure or possible deception?

- **Ability to hide the facts?**
  Is the disability going to become obvious to the employer during the process of checking references and employment verification?

- **Is the truth better?**
  Are there going to be signals given off that cause the employer to wonder anyway and perhaps cause the employer not to hire the individual?

- **Is the truth relevant?**
  For disabilities having no impact on the individual at work there is no reason to share the information. The Americans with Disabilities Act (ADA) makes the assumption that the presence of a disability is irrelevant, unless it clearly affects the person's ability to do the essential parts of the job.

- **Can the facts be checked?**
  In the case of a convicted felon trying to get a position within a company where security checks are standard procedure, the truth will come out and then the cover-up may be judged harshly.

- **Effects on the person?**
  For some, disclosure is a part of honest interactions, and they are too uncomfortable to carry the burden of nondisclosure around.

- **Consequences?**
  What are the ramifications of disclosure? While some employers are fearful of hiring people with previously hidden disabilities, some are not. Some hidden disabilities are more discriminated against than others (e.g., mental illness is often feared and misperceived).

Part of the job developer's role is to counsel job seekers with hidden disabilities regarding disclosure. Remember, it is not the job developer's job to decide for people. It is to take job seekers through a decision making process, weighing the above factors, so job seekers arrive at their own decisions. Once the person decides, the job developer must respect that decision and work with the individual accordingly on how to implement that decision. Should the choice be made to disclose, the individual may need advice as to how, when, and to whom to disclose.

The timing of the disclosure is also a personal decision. Since we know that employment discrimi-

---

GUIDELINES FOR A GOOD DISCLOSURE

1. Script your disclosure. Write it down and have it critiqued. Run through it with friends who are employers and with other people in the working world.

2. Rehearse your disclosure script until you feel comfortable and good about it, not only with your words, but with your body language.

3. When you prepare your script, avoid being too clinical or too detailed. It may be of great interest to you, but the interviewer wants to know only three things: Will you be there? Can you do the job as well or better than anyone else? Will you be of value to the company?

4. Remember your script and be positive about your skills and abilities. The more positive you are, the more you will convey that you are you and "just happen to have a disability." Conversely, the more you discuss your disability, the more important it will become in the employer's mind.

nation still occurs, many professionals feel that it is best to wait for the job offer. This depends on individual circumstances and preferences. After the offer, the timing of the disclosure will depend on the need for accommodations as well as the preferences of the worker. (Accommodations are discussed at length in Chapter 7.)

Consider whether the information will be better received after the employer has had the opportunity to get to know the worker independently of the disability label. If there is a probationary period for the position, the individual may wish to disclose after the completion of the probation.

Should there be no need for immediate accommodation, there is no rush and potentially no need to disclose to the employer. Finally, if the person decides he or she wants to let the employer know, carefully consider who should be told. There may be co-workers, supervisors, managers, human resources staff, or an Equal Employment Opportunities officer. Should they all be told or only a few of them?

Generally, begin by telling only those who need to know and let the others get to know the person first. Again, though, this is a personal decision. There are very few situations where everyone needs

---

PRESENTING PEOPLE WITH DISABILITIES

SKILLS, PERSONALITY, AND INTERESTS:
The goal is to highlight the selling points and talk about the skills, interests, and positive attributes of the person.

FUNCTIONAL LANGUAGE THAT PROMOTES SOLUTIONS:
Use terms that relate to employers such as job applicant, job description, and work force. Avoid jargon.

DON'T VOLUNTEER NEGATIVE INFORMATION:
Employers don't need help in finding negatives.

ORIENTED TO INDIVIDUAL EMPLOYER:
In order to meet employer needs, ask questions and investigate behind the scenes.

AGREED UPON BY JOB SEEKER:
The job seeker must be involved, informed, and in agreement with job development activities. Job development efforts must be based on the needs, interests, and desires of the job seeker.

PAST VS. PRESENT:
Contrasting past with present means explaining how the past problems have been addressed and what's happening now that demonstrates abilities.

RESPECT/CONFIDENTIALITY:
It is important to remember that when you are doing job development, you are modeling behavior for the employer. How you talk about and interact with the job seeker shows your level of respect for that person. Employers often will look to the job developer for leadership or a role model for future interactions.

CONFIDENCE AND COMMITMENT:
The employer will judge the candidate by how much he or she feels the job developer believes in and respects the job seeker. The job developer sets the tone with confidence and commitment.

HONESTY:
Honesty is important in developing long-term employer relationships. Nobody can make guarantees. The most able employee has had a job that did not work out. It is important not to make promises, but if you make them, see them through.

FOLLOW-UP:
Follow-up with employers is crucial. It's good customer service!

to know. Many employees opt to tell their supervisor or manager and a human resources representative. They later decide who among their co-workers to tell. This allows relationships to develop prior to disclosure and thus diminishes stigma.

Interviews

The time, energy, and resources that go into the mere act of getting an appointment for a job interview can be enormous. But now the real work begins. First, the job seeker must create a positive impression during the interview to maximize the chances of employment.

The job interview is the critical link in the job-seeking process. By agreeing to an interview, the employer is acknowledging an interest in hiring the applicant and the job seeker meets at least the general criteria for the position. It is now the job seeker's responsibility to prove to the employer that he or she is better qualified for the position than other candidates.

Part of the job developer's responsibility includes preparing the person for the standard interview scenario that any job applicant is subject to, as well as handling situations that may arise in relation to the person's disability. The issue of disclosure, already discussed in this section, needs to be addressed with the job seeker. As noted already, there are legal rights that an individual has under the Americans with Disabilities Act (ADA), and also state laws applying to employment. The ADA clearly prohibits an employer from asking about a disability. But there are also practical realities of the interview situation as outlined here.

For persons with physical disabilities or sensory impairments, the need to request accommodations for the interview virtually eliminates the choice about disclosure. The only decision to be made is that of timing. Should disclosure occur when the interview is being set up or should it occur "naturally" when the interview takes place?

There are less clear cases in which an individual may display behavior or have physical characteristics that are perceived by the potential employer as "unusual" and could be misinterpreted. Is it better to leave unanswered questions in the employer's mind, or to try and clear up the misconceptions or fears that the employer may have about the disability? Or, an individual's disability may pose communication challenges that can be an obstacle to conveying an individual's qualifications for a job. Should an advocate accompany the person on the interview to assist with communication?

There is no one right answer for every situation. You have to make the "best guess" about the impact it will have on the hiring decision and the person's success on the job.

The ultimate determinant is the preference of the person with a disability, but it is the job developer's role to assist the job seeker in weighing the pros and cons of pursuing various strategies.

EMPLOYMENT PROVISIONS: THE AMERICANS WITH DISABILITIES ACT

- applies to all employers with fifteen or more employees

PRE-EMPLOYMENT INQUIRIES
- no disability-related questions verbally or in writing
- questions only on job requirements
- no medical examinations prior to offer of employment
- medical examinations allowed after offer of employment only if required of all employees in job category

QUALIFIED INDIVIDUAL
an individual with a disability who, with or without reasonable accommodation, can perform the essential functions of the employment position that such individual holds or desires

ESSENTIAL FUNCTIONS OF A JOB
- whether position exists to perform that function
- # of other employees available to perform function
- degree of expertise or skill required based on written job description, position history, time spent performing function, and consequences of not performing function

NON-DISCRIMINATION
Under the Americans with Disabilities Act of 1990, employers cannot discriminate
on the basis of disability against qualified individuals with disabilities regarding:
- recruitment, advertising, and job application procedures
- hiring, upgrading, promotion, award of tenure, demotion, transfer, layoff, termination, right of return from layoff, and rehiring
- rates of pay or any other form of compensation and changes in compensation
- job assignments, job classifications, organizational structures, position descriptions, lines of progressions, and seniority lists
- leaves of absence, sick leave, or any other leave
- fringe benefits available by virtue of employment, whether or not administered by the organization
- selection and financial support for training, including: apprenticeships, professional meetings, conferences and other related activities, and selection for leaves of absence to pursue training
- activities sponsored by an employer, including social and recreational programs
- any other term, condition, or privilege of employment

Source: US Equal Employment Opportunity Commission's 29 CFR Part 1630
Equal Employment Opportunities for Individuals with Disabilities Final Rule, July 26, 1991

DEALING OPENLY WITH DISABILITY

- Describe by qualifications, not disability.
- Stress positive current activity.
- Don't volunteer negative information.
- Avoid medical terms or jargon.
- Connect problem with significant life event.
- Stress being in charge and control.
- Past problem vs. present capability.
- Disability is not equal to work skills.

While the ADA clearly states that a potential employer cannot ask questions concerning a person's disability, this does not necessarily stop employers from making such inquiries, even if inadvertently. It is part of the job developer's responsibility to make the job seeker aware of their legal rights and to discuss ways of responding to intrusive inquiries in a way that minimizes the negative impact on the interview.

For example, if an employer asks, "What's wrong with you?," the individual could respond by saying, "You can't ask me that. It's illegal under the ADA." This is correct, but may result in the person's not being hired.

A better response would be: "I'll tell you what — let me tell you all the things I can do," and then go on to describe why the person is qualified for the job. Obviously if an employer is persistent in asking about a person's disability, and the person chooses not to disclose, inform the employer gently that such inquiries are illegal.

It is important that people with disabilities know and exercise their legal rights. But such rights need to be used in a proactive way to promote the individual for the position. While people with disabilities certainly should file actions under the ADA when they have been clearly discriminated against, the ADA should be used more as an education tool and not as a sledge hammer. The goal is to get jobs, not file lawsuits. The main objective with interview strategies is to determine the best course of action so that the person not only gets the job, but succeeds on the job.

The manner in which a disability is explained or accommodations are requested, including the words used, can have enormous impact on the perception that is created of the person's capabilities. In the insular world of the disability field, jargon and medical terms are used freely. There is a need to find ways to talk about disability with the general public in terms that enhance, rather than obscure, understanding. This field also is accustomed to fully accepting people with disabilities as individuals. Try to put yourself in the "employer's shoes" and realize that there are still enormous preconceived notions and stereotypes, fear, and in some cases outright prejudice against people with disabilities that need to be overcome.

CONSIDERATIONS IN INTERVIEWING

- How well can the applicant present information and respond to questions?
- What are the applicant's preferences?
- How much information should you give ahead of time?
- Is an alternative format needed? What's appropriate?
- Should you be present during the interview? If so, how do you positively explain your role?
- How active should you be in the interview and how does this impact the employer's perception of the applicant?
- What are the strategies for involving the applicant who has limited or no verbal skills?
- What to do when interview is going poorly? If the employer or applicant is uncomfortable?

A simple illustration of stereotyping comes from looking at "mental illness" and "mental retardation." While anyone who is familiar with these disabilities understands the distinction between the two and the diversity of individuals to whom such terms apply, the general public (including employers) often will use these terms interchangeably. They may have preconceived notions about what they mean as a result of their limited exposure to people with disabilities. Such exposure has often been via the media, which has tended to perpetuate fears and stereotypes about people with disabilities.

Interview Accommodations

There may be accommodations needed for a successful interview, and some of these are fairly obvious. If a person is in a wheelchair, the interview location, including the rest room, must be accessible. If the job seeker has difficulty communicating due to a hearing impairment or speech impediment, some alternative method of communication must be used, such as an interpreter.

What if the person simply interviews poorly, possibly due to cognitive limitations? What if testing is a standard part of the interview process for the job, and the person tests poorly? Possible accommodations under these circumstances could be: an alternative testing format, a situational assessment (i.e., a short-term job tryout for a day or two before a final hiring decision is made), or being hired on a trial basis.

The job developer or job seeker will have to advocate for this type of accommodation with the employer, requesting it as a reasonable accommodation under the ADA. Such strategies should be used judiciously, and only in cases where the standard interviewing and hiring procedures put the individual at a disadvantage.

There are always pluses and minuses to using any type of accommodation for interviews. The decision of whether to request an interview accommodation should depend on how much the accommodation will positively impact the chances of the individual getting the job versus the potential negative impact of using such an accommodation. If an interview accommodation is necessary, the job developer or job seeker should explain the accommodation to the employer.

For example, if an interpreter is to be used, the specifics of interpreter etiquette (such as directing questions at the individual and not the interpreter) should be discussed ahead of time. Remember that an employer may have never used such an accommodation before. It is important to emphasize how an accommodation will assist the employer in making an educated hiring decision.

REQUESTING ACCOMMODATIONS FOR INTERVIEWING

• Have the person agree to accommodation request ahead of time.
• Explain the purpose of the accommodation.
• Illustrate how the employer can make a more informed hiring decision.
• Acknowledge and respond to employer concerns.
• Explain accommodation in nontechnical language.

Interview Strategies

Interviewers are extremely varied in their styles, approaches, and ability to accurately determine the capabilities of an individual. Some interviewers will use a very structured format that solicits specific information. Other interviewers use an open-ended style that requires the job seeker to take the initiative in providing information.

SUCCESSFUL JOB INTERVIEWS

• Prepare the employer in advance with what to expect, including your role.
• Modify the interview as necessary.
• Work with the applicant and family/residence on dress and grooming.
• Follow up with both the applicant and the employer on positives and negatives.
• Practice interviewing.
• Arrive early.

Interviews can be a few simple questions, such as "Where have you worked? and "How soon can you start?" Interviews also can consist of open-ended ("Tell me about yourself") or fairly abstract questions. Group interviews, in which the individual is interviewed not only by the supervisor but also by potential co-workers, also are becoming more common.

Job seekers and job developers should be ready for the varied styles of interviews. Discuss and practice how to handle various scenarios. Before the interview, determine the information that is essential to share with the interviewer (i.e., the individual's strengths and how he or she could benefit the employer). Then you can develop strategies for communicating this information, no matter what the format.

Since interviews can vary greatly, it's important for job seekers (and job developers as well) to practice interview skills. Informational interviews done strictly for learning about a company or business and not to get a job and mock interviews done with actual employers at their place of business are good strategies to give job seekers practice in interviewing. Such practice techniques are particularly helpful if the person is looking for his or her first job, or hasn't undertaken a job search in many years.

DISCLOSURE OF A HIDDEN DISABILITY

PROS

1. Reduction of stress. Many people report that "hiding is more stressful than telling." Disclosing also makes it easier, if the need arises, to discuss accommodations.
2. Immediate knowledge of the environment you will be in. You will have "cleared the air" and will know what to expect.
3. Release from the worry that a past employer or reference might inadvertently "drop" the fact that you have a disability.
4. Full freedom to examine and question health insurance and other benefits. For certain disabilities, if a medical examination is required, you will not have to worry about passing it.
5. Freedom to communicate with your employer if you face changes in your condition.
6. Disclosure may make you feel more "comfortable." That word is the real key to the issue of disclosure.

CONS

1. Bad past experience(s): rejection or loss of a job because of the disability.
2. Fear of being placed in a "dead-end job."
3. Fear of being an object of curiosity.
4. Fear that if something doesn't go right, it will be blamed on the disability.
5. Fear of being "different."
6. Fear of not getting the job.
7. Raises other questions for employers.
8. May trigger stereotyping.

Exercise 5-A
Marketing a Product

Purpose: To provide an opportunity to practice marketing skills with a focus on presenting information in a positive and creative way.

Directions:

1. Choose an item to promote. It can be anything from a candy bar to a car. You can work individually or in a group.
2. Spend five minutes deciding on your approach. What is the product you are going to market and what approach will the group use?
3. Spend five minutes planning your words and actions. What will each person say and do?
4. Make a presentation in front of another group. If in a group, everyone must say a portion of the presentation.

• What did you like about the presentation? What worked?

• How did you determine your overall approach to take in marketing the product?

• What is the purpose of this exercise?

Exercise 5-B
Case Studies in Presenting Individuals

Purpose: To help critically evaluate your role in marketing an individual to an employer, to think about preparing an individual for an interview and possibly intervening with the employer, and to maintain respect for the individual and his or her right to privacy while ensuring a successful interview.

Instructions: Read through each case and answer the questions listed.

Case Study: Chris

Chris is a thirty-year-old man with multiple diagnoses of schizophrenia, substance abuse, and significant learning disabilities. Due to the learning difficulties, he was placed in special education classes in second grade. Disorientation, mood swings, and auditory hallucinations first started to occur at age thirteen, and he was hospitalized soon after. Medication compliance and family support were problematic, and Chris was placed in a residential treatment program at age sixteen. He remained there until age twenty-one. Since that time he has had six hospitalizations. (The last hospitalization was six months ago.) He also has been placed twice in a detoxification program and currently participates in a day treatment program. He sees a psychiatrist every two weeks and lives in a supervised apartment program where he receives twenty-four-hour-a-day staff supervision and support. He is currently on probation for an armed robbery conviction. His family lives nearby, and he maintains occasional contact with his mother and younger sister. (His brother is in jail and father is deceased.)

His previous work history consists of a series of entry-level food service and cleaning jobs, which he obtained with the help of family and his former case manager. He also attended McWorkshop Industries (a sheltered workshop) for three months in 1988. The report from the workshop states that Chris reads at less than a second grade level and has negligible math skills. He is very engaging and outgoing, though overly boisterous at times. His interests include rap music, partying with his "friends," and playing and watching basketball. He has said he would like to work in a music or video store, or get an office job that pays well. He is a high priority person for you to help find a job since his funding for the day treatment program will soon be ending and his current living situation is dependent on being involved in a work or therapeutic program.

1. Identify a potential employer that would match Chris's interests and skills.
2. Decide how to present Chris to a potential employer. Using the information you would have available to you (Chris' self-report, discharge summary, treatment plan, workshop report of performance, and psychological evaluation), embellish upon the provided details and decide what you want to highlight about Chris.
3. Prepare a brief one-to-two-minute presentation on Chris to answer the employer's question, "Can you tell me a little about Chris?"

Once an interview has been arranged:
4. How would the question of disclosure be handled? Would disclosure happen? If so, when?
5. What should your role be for the interview?
6. What should you work on with Chris to prepare him for the interview?

Case Study: Denise

Denise is a woman in her mid-thirties who has suffered a traumatic brain injury as a result of a car accident. Prior to the accident, she had obtained a college degree and worked in middle management in the banking industry. After the accident, Denise spent six months in a coma. She has significant cognitive and physical limitations. These include:

- *short-term memory loss*
- *slow and slurred speech*
- *an ability to walk only short distances*
- *low frustration tolerance*
- *tendency to emotional outbursts, with yelling and screaming*

Denise has recently completed a computer training program. With support, she did well in the program. Denise has applied for a position at a local hospital, and is scheduled for an initial interview for an opening in the medical billing department. Determine a plan of action for how to maximize her chances for success in the interview.

Questions:

1. Should you intervene prior to the interview with the supervisor. If so, what would you do?

2. What types of accommodations might be requested for the interview?

3. What should be disclosed, if anything?

4. Should you sit in on the interview, and what should your role be if you do so?

5. What should you work with Denise on, to prepare her for the interview?

6

Marketing Materials and Tools

This book focuses on what to say and do when contacting and negotiating with employers, because effective job development is about relationship building. However, this chapter addresses marketing materials and other tools a job developer uses in marketing and job development activities. Marketing materials include information a job developer gives an employer such as business cards, resumes, letters, brochures, flyers, fact sheets, and letters of support. Other tools, such as a Rolodex and tickler files, support your marketing activities.

First, a word of caution. The key to job development is getting out and talking to employers and marketing potential employees. Marketing involves action and follow-up. The materials you use are simply tools to facilitate the process and provide information to employers.

Do not fixate on details of marketing materials at the expense of time spent on job development. Create materials and use them, then revise them as needed. They are not museum pieces of art, but rather supplements of day-to-day work.

These guidelines for developing and using marketing materials are based on feedback from formal focus groups of employers representing human resources, marketing, and disability management, in conjunction with the extensive experiences of the authors in working with employers. Approaches suggested to help start off well with employers are:

- Use clearly and concisely written materials.
- Eliminate typographical errors.
- Target marketing materials to employers' needs using business language.
- Avoid stigmatizing characterizations (in words and images).
- Eliminate jargon that is unfamiliar to those outside of the disability field.

Marketing materials are used to get the attention and interest of the desired audience and leave them wanting more information. If written materials are too long, they will not get read. They need to be attention-grabbing, concise, and free from typos. Target language to the particular audience to keep their attention. Many organizations try to save money by having one piece of general marketing material for everyone including consumers, families, employers, and other professionals. These groups all have differing needs and expectations.

Organizations should have brochures or information sheets targeted to specific audiences. Carefully proofread all materials and have others not involved in the writing proofread them as well. Agencies should take advantage of the relationships they have with businesses and involve their business partners in the development and review of marketing materials. Since business is the target audience, they can provide real expertise on what should (and should not) be included.

MARKETING TOOLS

- brochures
- resumes
- business card
- pens/pencils
- Rolodex
- placement stats
- letter from CEO
- cover letters
- thank-you letters
- fact/info sheets
- calendars
- computer Rolodex
- reference letters
- customer testimony

Above is a sampling of typical marketing materials. What is used in job development activities is less important than the quality and timeliness of the efforts. Bad marketing materials or poor follow-up are worse than no marketing materials.

Resumes

The rules concerning resumes for people with disabilities are the same as for everyone else. There are a variety of resources available on resume formats. (Check the business section of the local bookstore or library.)

Some jobs do not require a resume. What are the pros and cons of having one? If a resume is helpful for job seekers to have (i.e., they need them for the type of job they seek or it is an accommodation for filling out applications) then developing one is a good idea. But if a resume serves no purpose, don't waste time on one.

For example, most retail stores and fast food establishments don't expect applicants to come in with resumes for entry level positions. However, if an individual is applying for a job in an office setting, a resume would be expected. A resume can be particularly helpful to highlight the strengths of individuals for whom personal interactions are a challenge due to a physical disability or cognitive challenges. This is true even of work settings in which resumes are not traditionally used. Whatever the case, a resume should be developed quickly and should not detract from time spent on job search/job development activities.

What if a person has limited experience or major gaps in work history? A traditional resume would call attention to such "weaknesses." In those cases, a functional resume that highlights the skills rather than the work experience of the individual would make sense.

Also, there are a number of creative methods to downplay gaps in experience and work history: using only years not months for work dates; not distinguishing between paid and unpaid work; and giving a brief summary (in positive terms) about what the person was doing when he or she wasn't working. Using a nontraditional format probably implies that something is awry, but it at least allows the applicant to put a spotlight on strengths, not deficits.

Another alternative is to abandon the standard resume format. Instead, use a personal profile of the individual, pinpointing his or her abilities, skills, and interests. This type of format can be particularly useful for individuals with limited work experience. A personal profile can help the employer see past the disability and start viewing the person as an individual with various interests and abilities.

The purpose of a resume is to be a marketing tool. It should not tell a person's life story. Instead, think of it as an "advertisement" for a person intended to get the employer's attention and move the job search forward. The assets are highlighted and potential negatives are omitted.

TIPS FOR RESUMES

- Highlight the positives: A resume is a place to boast about experience.
- Make it easy to find information, skills, and experience. A person is lucky if his or her resume gets thirty seconds of someone's attention. Make information easy to find.
- Use nontechnical language. For some jobs, technical language is okay, but beware of including too much jargon.
- Use enough information to create interest. The goal is to summarize skills and experience but not overwhelm the reader.
- Leave the reader wanting to find out more. People get jobs by having interviews. A resume that piques curiosity and leaves the reader intrigued gets the job seeker one step closer to employment.
- Have a natural progression. A resume should make good employment sense.
- Avoid "red flags." Red flags are signs of potential flaws in applicants.
- Have a clean appearance. Most people prefer to read information that is clear and concise.
- Resumes should be one page unless the person has such extensive publications, professional affiliations, and accomplishments that this is impossible. If a resume is truly targeted, it should be possible to present the information on one page.
- Use proper grammar and spelling. There is no excuse for such mistakes in this era of spell checkers and grammar checkers. It is worth the time.

References

References also can be useful in a successful job search. The rules for references for people with disabilities are no different than those for any other job seeker. Many people initially may feel that they don't know anyone they could put down as a reference. In the process of planning and identifying personal networks, you may come across individuals who would be helpful as references, such as a politician or well-connected business executive who is a friend of the family.

These connections can be exceedingly helpful. Every effort should be made to get beyond the world of human services for reference names. Some jobs require references; others do not. If a person has strong references, such as someone well-known (for positive reasons) in the community, you certainly should volunteer references. Otherwise, give references only at the request of the employer.

Bad references are worse than none at all. It is important to make sure people can say positive things before they are listed as references, and that they have given their permission. It is helpful for job developers to check the references themselves, to ensure that they are positive and not a hindrance in a successful job search. Checking references also can prevent the inadvertent disclosure of a disability by one of the references.

Business Cards

Business cards are the most basic of marketing tools and the most common mode of exchanging names, addresses, and phone numbers in the business world. They end up in people's pockets and serve as reminders.

They should be carried at all times and generously given out. Give each employer one during your initial meeting. Cards should include as much information as possible:
- name
- phone
- title
- fax
- TTY
- e-mail address
- web site address

GUIDELINES FOR WRITTEN MARKETING TOOLS

- no typos
- no jargon
- addressed to your audience
- positive image
- logo/organization name clear
- eye appealing
- state what you offer
- clear and concise
- local focus

Brochures

Brochures convey messages in many ways. Cover graphics or artwork send a message, which may be subtle or obvious. An example is a wheelchair on the cover of a brochure, which may convey the message that all potential employees will have physical disabilities.

Next comes the inside message. Many organizations attempt to list everything about who they are and what they do. Keep to the main points. There is plenty of time for details in a meeting.

You need to get the brochures into the hands of the right people, and have enough information to pique interest and make them say, "Hmmm, I should give them a call. I want to know more..." You can offer more details during in-person meetings or when more information is requested. Anything promised in a brochure should be available if requested, such as job coaching, guaranteed supervision, or staff coverage.

Cover Letters

Send all resumes with cover letters. Failing to do so is the surest way to have a resume thrown out. Ideally the paper should match that of the resume. All should be typed and presented neatly. They help tie the resume to the potential job and highlight how the job seeker has the experience and qualifications for the job.

COVER LETTER FORMAT

Paragraph #1: Position title and how you heard about it.

Paragraph #2: Summarize relevant skills.

Paragraph #3: Restate interest/qualifications and say when follow-up will happen.

It is helpful to develop several templates for cover letters, so you can use them as a starting point for future letters.

Thank-You Letters

Thank-you letters make good business sense. In addition to being a sign of social skills, it is a way to remind an employer of the points made or intended to be made during the meeting. Send them after all interviews and marketing meetings.

THANK-YOU LETTER FORMAT

Paragraph #1: Express appreciation for time. Mention position title and date. Confirm your interest in the job.

Paragraph #2: Review your relevant skills. Personalize.

Paragraph #3: Express desire to be considered. Offer thanks again.

Other Helpful Materials

Fact Sheets
Good for expanding on information in brochures or focusing on a specific topic. Some examples: a fact sheet on jobs/tasks in a specific industry, information on financial incentives, and a step-by-step outline of the placement process.

Picture Books
Showing people your agency has previously placed, working in a variety of settings with a short caption under each picture, can spark the interest of employers who are unfamiliar with community employment for people with significant disabilities.

Letters of Reference
From satisfied employers on their letterhead

Newsletters
May include information on job candidates, recent placements, profiles of employers, and tips and trends in the business and disability field.

Rolodex cards
With your agency information

"Giveaways"
Pens, memo pads, coffee mugs

Flyers
Announcements of special training events

Posters
Depictions of workplace diversity

Press Releases
Business items of interest related to your services, labor trends, etc.

Annual Reports
A review that highlights your successes in serving the business community

QUESTIONS IN DEVELOPING MATERIALS

• What is the purpose of the material?
• What is the message you want to convey?
• What needs to be included or excluded?
• Who is the audience?
• What kind of format do you want to use? Size? Color and type of paper?

Remember that marketing materials are intended to pique interest and be part of an overall marketing package. All marketing materials should convey a positive image about people with disabilities and not reinforce stereotypes. Give examples of diverse jobs and employers. If you use pictures or illustrations, use a variety of settings, with people portrayed as naturally fitting into the work environment.

Don't try to be the expert on marketing materials. Use the businesses you deal with, particularly those with marketing departments and marketing experts, to help with creation and design of marketing materials.

Printing and desktop publishing companies also can be helpful. Once you have developed draft versions of materials, get feedback from a variety of businesses. Not only will you get help, but this can also be a good way of developing relationships with businesses.

Financing Marketing Materials

Some strategies for extending your budget:

- Get a local employer with an in-house printing operation to produce your materials.

- Get a grant from a local foundation or service group to defray the costs of materials.

While good marketing materials are helpful, your personal interactions with employers are a much greater key to your success. Good personal interactions can make up for bad (or no) marketing materials. Good materials are not going to make up for ineffective personal interactions.

Exercise 6-A
Critiquing Marketing Materials

Purpose: To provide an opportunity to critique marketing materials and discuss lessons learned, highlighting stronger and weaker materials.

Instructions: Work with another person from an agency similar to yours. Each person should share any marketing materials he or she uses (business cards, brochures, etc.) with the group. Focus on issues such as clarity and brevity. Offer feedback on ways they might be improved upon. What should be highlighted as positive aspects of the marketing materials?

If there are no real materials to critique, design a brochure aimed at employers or plan an entire marketing kit. Decide what should be in a marketing kit for a job developer's first meeting with employers. This will not be targeted at a specific community. Plan the look of the cover as well as the formatting of the inside.

7

Securing the Deal

his section presents a framework for developing relationships with employers. It will help you think about the timing of employer negotiations. Discussion will focus on what information, services, and supports to offer the employer and the impact on whether or not the job seeker is hired and the quality of the work experience. It provides both a theoretical framework for negotiating and practical experience in small and large group exercises and role playing.

Once you make the initial contact with an employer, you should have a strategy to convince the employer to hire the job applicant. Sometimes staff who are new or uncomfortable with job development might try to get the process over with as quickly as possible (preferably on the first contact). Like anyone pressured into making a quick decision, the employer may pull back and say no because he or she is not ready to make a commitment. (Think about someone dealing with a car salesperson who says the decision must be made today in order to get a special deal.)

The aim is not to slow down the job development process but to be sensitive to the needs of different employers and vary the approach accordingly. If an employer offers to interview the job applicant that afternoon and makes a job offer on that first interview, that's wonderful.

Unfortunately, this doesn't happen often very often. Be cautious about pushing prematurely during the first contact to have the applicant interviewed or asking the employer to make a hiring decision after the initial interview. If an employer feels pushed too hard too fast, the result may be the termination of all negotiations with the job developer now and in the future.

One way to think about timing employer negotiations is to use the analogy between "courting an employer" and the dating process in personal relationships. Dividing the "courting" process into stages can help a job developer think about what to say or do during successive interactions with employers.

Comparing a first meeting with a new employer to a first date can provide a framework for deciding when and how much commitment to ask for from an employer. During the early stages, when minimal trust or credibility has been established, asking for a commitment (i.e., meeting a date's parents or pushing a reluctant employer to interview a candidate right away) may result in discomfort that pushes the other party away. Each employer, just like each job developer, will have different boundaries and comfort levels that affect how fast the person progresses in relationship building, making commitments, and taking risks. This analogy helps to maintain perspective about the relationship building process with employers that a customer service approach requires.

The first interaction with an employer should be one in which the job developer gathers information about the organization.

INFORMATION TO GATHER DURING THE FIRST MEETING

- the product or service delivered
- the number of employees and the types of jobs they have
- areas of turnover and reasons for the turnover
- busy seasons; staffing problems
- areas of growth or future staffing needs
- needs for any information or resources
- past or present experiences with employees with disabilities

63

While you can't obtain all of the information at one time, you should do it early on. Job developers also should be prepared with general information about their organization's capacity to meet many of the personnel needs of the workplace. Whether or not the issue of disability is discussed, all interactions must be positive and highlight the assets of the job applicant. As with any good salesperson, the job developer must be able to market the product (the job applicant) with confidence and persistence.

INHERENT SELLING POINTS

- skills, experience, attributes, and personality of the job seeker
- past successes of the program
- promotion by satisfied employers
- agency expertise
- assistance/information to business
- professional knowledge of applicant
- community service/contribution
- good public relations

Whether the courtship and negotiations with an employer are done quickly or over time, at some point the employer is likely to raise concerns or objections that can stall or halt the process. Communicating to employers an understanding of their needs and concerns will help build trust. Job development staff also must be able to help employers see how their concerns can be addressed successfully and their employment needs met through hiring these job applicants.

ASSESSING EMPLOYERS' NEEDS AND CONCERNS

- Listen first.
- Ask about current and future employment needs.
- Ask about previous experience. with people with disabilities.
- Ask about previous experience with agencies.
- Describe ideal/troublesome employee.
- Talk to human resources, managers, and front line employees.
- Identify gaps and inefficiencies.

Some new job developers offer employers everything up front as an enticement to hiring the job applicant. As with the inexperienced buyer at an auction, the end result can be a bad deal.

HOW TO RESPOND TO OBJECTIONS

- Listen actively.
- Repeat /clarify.
- Acknowledge concerns.
- Offer information.
- Gaining assent.

"Employers as Partners," a monograph by Charles Galloway (1982), provides a useful framework for negotiating strategy.[6] It divides offerings to employers into three categories: inherent selling points, sweeteners, and hole cards. *Inherent selling points* are the positive attributes of the applicant or program or services. These may include the skills, experience, and positive personality traits of the applicant, successful job placement and retention rates of the program, personal and work references for the applicant, a list of satisfied employers who have hired workers from your agency, and consultation offered to supervisors and co-workers to assist them in hiring and training workers with disabilities. These things are mentioned or offered to all potential employers up front and carry no stigma or downside with respect to the applicant or agency.

Sweeteners and *hole cards* are services or options offered to an employer to help close a deal, but only if needed. These may include initial or long-term job coaching, monetary incentives such as on the job training funds, starting the worker on a temporary basis or on an agency's payroll, or guaranteeing production.

SWEETENERS AND HOLE CARDS

- situational assessment
- on the job training (VR, ARC, or other funding sources)
- WOTC or other tax credits
- initial job coaching
- employer or co-worker stipend
- temporary work assignment
- pre-screened applicants
- contract work (on agency payroll)
- promising supervision
- promising productivity (job will get done)
- Dept. of Labor waiver

These would not be offered initially because each carries a risk in terms of how the applicant is perceived, the potential for lower wages, social isolation, lack of investment by the employer, and the over-commitment of agency services and resources. They can be used, but carefully and with full knowledge of the ramifications of their use.

To help apply this to your organization, write down what services your agency typically offers employers. Using inherent selling points, sweeteners, and hole cards as a framework, analyze if and when you should offer these services in the negotiation process, and what the potential benefits and ramifications could be for each service. Another variation of this is to look at the agency brochure and see what employer benefits and services are listed. Use the categories above to analyze these features regarding whether they are *inherent selling points, sweeteners,* or *hole cards.* Discuss if these features should be listed in a brochure.

Employer Supports and Accommodations

Once you have identified possible employment opportunities, look more closely at the work environment. Assess the resources and supports available, both on and off the job, to figure out what can be changed through removal or augmentation to make this a successful job. Assessing the work culture and supports available in the workplace is important for both successful job performance and social inclusion and acceptance of the worker. Developing accommodations and supports is an integral part of the skill and knowledge base that the job developer brings to the task of finding jobs. Successful job development involves fitting the job to the person as much as fitting the person to the job.

IS THIS THE RIGHT JOB?

• Does it meet the applicant's quality standards?
• What can we do to change the environment (restructure or modify job)?
• What can we do to add supports (change resources)?
• What can we do to change the person's skills or behavior (train)?

The employment aspects of the Americans with Disabilities Act (ADA) pertaining to interviews were reviewed in Chapter 5. Job developers should have strong working knowledge of the employment aspects (Title I) of the ADA, not only concerning pre-employment inquiries, but also concerning reasonable accommodations. In essence, the ADA states that employers are required to make reasonable accommodations for an employee with a disability, as long as the accommodation does not pose an "undue hardship" to the employer. Factors considered in whether an accommodation poses an undue hardship include:

- the nature and cost of the accommodation
- the resources and size of the business
- the type of business including composition, functions, and structure of the workforce
- the impact the accommodation would have on the facility and business as whole

REASONABLE ACCOMMODATIONS

• required for applicants and workers with disabilities (at the employers expense)
• when such accommodations would not impose undue hardship

By definition, accommodation is individual and job specific, so exact categorizations are hard to come by. For this reason, think of reasonable accommodation as essentially relating either to the job itself or the supervision provided. Examples of supervisory accommodation include:

- providing work requests and specifications of tasks in writing
- making a concerted effort to give positive feedback more often or more explicitly
- soliciting a worker's self evaluation before providing critical feedback
- applying work policies such as sick leave, break schedules, and time schedule flexibility
- providing more individual training, directly or with outside assistance
- providing a co-worker mentor to help the person become integrated into the workforce

Examples of job accommodation include:
- changing the worker's office by a move or simple construction (e.g., partitions)
- changing the worker's schedule due to personal disability-related characteristics (e.g., lack of concentration) or treatment needs (therapy appointments)

ACCOMMODATION EXAMPLES

Admin. Assistant (psychiatric disability), concentration and memory problems.
Solution: soothing music in one earphone and taped instruction to augment written materials in the other ear. ($150)

Policeman (learning disability), difficulty taking standard civil service tests.
Solution: 50% more time and allowed to use dictionary for exam. ($0)

Senior programmer (learning disability), difficulty with memory and using correct wording.
Solution: e-mail to facilitate communication. Computer software for word prediction and grammar check. Voice output equipment. ($1750)

Repair person (psychiatric disability), difficulty attending to training seminars. Cannot take notes while listening to presentation.
Solution: co-worker carbon copies notes (or photocopy) (<$10)

Computer programmer (head injury), inability to read past the vertical midline of computer screen, starting on the left side.
Solution: software package that splits the screen and display the text on the left side. ($600)

Clerk-typist (depression and alcoholism), problems with quantity and quality of her work.
Solution: extended sick leave covering hospitalization. Flexible schedule to accommodate weekly therapy. ($0)

Receiving clerk (congenital heart defect and mobility limits due to childhood polio), job requires unpacking merchandise, checking it in, and making price checks.
Solution: rolling chair with locking wheels, adjustable to the level of the task. ($200)

Well-drilling rig operator (back injury), vibration irritates back.
Solution: adjustable mechanical seat absorbs most vibration. Used by all workers, preventing new problems. ($1100)

Electronics technician (AIDS), taking large amounts of time off/sick leave.
Solution: company allowed a flexible work schedule and redistributed portions of workload. Company began AIDS awareness training. ($0)

Telephone consultant (head injury), experiences memory loss and auditory discrimination problem. Job is to respond to requests for information and enter that data into the computer.
Solution: sound-absorbing office partitions to reduce noise/distractions, phone bell programmed to differentiate her phone. Antiglare screen to prevent fatigue and dizziness. Written instructions, schedules, etc. ($345)

Packager (attention deficit disorder), trouble staying on task.
Solution: tape recorder and headphones with cassettes of music and frequent reminders of tasks. (<$200)

Quick-service grill operator (learning disability), cannot read and can recognize only a few letters.
Solution: condiment bins coded. Key words used by staff and learned (flashcards) by chef for written orders. (<$25)

Data entry clerk (agoraphobia), trouble with rush-hour commute.
Solution: change hours for employee. ($0)

– Source: Job Accommodation Network

- changing the worker's job tasks through re-assignment of duties
- allowing the worker to work at home
- use of assistive technology, such as voice recognition software, modified computer keyboards, and other high-tech and low-tech devices
- job creation and job carving by making essentially a new job out of existing tasks done partially by others (See Chapter 8 for additional information on job creation.)
- sharing a job with another worker, either with a disability (as in transitional employment) or a co-worker without a disability who can serve as a paid supervisor to the worker or an unpaid, more informal, mentor

Any of these accommodations are best developed in a spirit of cooperation, not conflict, with employers. The law does not seek to impose demands on employers, particularly smaller ones, that might interfere with their ability to compete in the market economy. Even when accommodations are required, enforcement is often slow.

GUIDELINES ON REQUESTING ACCOMMODATIONS

Accommodation request = disclosure
When should request be made?
• needed as part of hiring process?
• needed immediately to perform job duties?
• impact of requesting:
- before hire
- immediately after
- waiting a month or more
Impact accommodation will have on workplace
Co-workers involved? Need to know?
Alternatives to accommodation
• more inclusive
• less stigmatizing
Is accommodation absolutely necessary?

It is incumbent upon advocates and people with disabilities alike to approach the concept of reasonable accommodation as a joint problem-solving exercise with many possible solutions to any one problem.

However, if circumstances warrant it, job developers and job seekers should not be hesitant to gen-tly remind employers that providing reasonable accommodations is not a "favor" to the potential employee, but rather something that the law requires of the employer.

COUNSELING JOB SEEKERS ON ACCOMMODATION REQUESTS

• Help identify needed accommodations.
• Discuss how the accommodation request will impact disclosure.
• Review the potential effect on workplace perceptions.
• Provide information on the ADA and how to use it pro-actively.
• Work on how the request will be made.

Requesting accommodations requires some level of disclosure concerning disability. As with any issue related to disclosure, the decision when to request an accommodation is subject to a variety of variables. Factors to consider include:

- Is the accommodation needed as part of the interview/hiring process?
- Is it needed immediately to perform job duties?
- What will be the impact of making the request before hiring, immediately after, or a month or more later?

As always with disclosure issues, adhere absolutely to the job seeker's wishes. However, part of the counseling role of employment staff is to assist the job seeker through the decision-making process, in order to consider the implications of disclosure and nondisclosure.

In the process of advocating for supports and accommodations, it is important that negotiations with employers don't have the unintentional effect of limiting employer support or involvement with the worker with a disability. Try asking the employer what initial training and support they offer new hires, and what adaptations or modifications to the existing training and supports they would be willing to offer the job applicant if needed.

If this is not sufficient, you may offer traditional job coaching or other supports in conjunction with the training and supports offered by the employer. Portray agency services and supports as a supplement rather than an alternative or replacement for the training and benefits the employer provides to employees.

NATURAL SUPPORTS IN THE WORKPLACE

• Support is a natural feature of the workplace.
• Each workplace has its own culture.
• Social integration comes first, not second.
• External support has multiple effects on the workplace.
• Ongoing support requires partnerships with business.

Recent research authored by David Mank and his colleagues clearly indicates the importance of considering social inclusion on the job development process. The findings stress the importance of maximizing employer supports, or using what is termed natural supports, and deviating from typical employer practices with caution.

The researchers found that if the job acquisition process, compensation, work role, and initial orientation and training for the person with a disability was similar to what was typical for that workplace, the person with a disability was more likely to be well-integrated into the workplace. If support for the person on the job was provided by co-workers, rather than an outside agency, the end result was higher wages and greater social integration.

Of particular importance for job developers, the researchers found that the level of integration did not improve over time. This is in contrast to the presumption that, even in cases where extensive agency support is provided when the job begins, as this support is faded, increased integration on the job will occur. The implication of this is that job developers should be cautious about offering high amounts of agency support. Instead, develop and design jobs so that workplace integration begins to occur day one on the job.

Developing accommodations and supports is an integral part of the job development process rather than something left to chance or thought about "after-the-fact." Using these strategies, you can find successful employment opportunities for people with more severe disabilities.

This means a job developer needs to have the orientation that his or her job is to search for or create opportunities for people to succeed. Don't waste time screening out individuals because of the nature or severity of their disability.

ELEMENTS OF WORKPLACE INTEGRATION
MANK, CIOFFI, AND YOVANOFF[7]
Oregon Natural Supports Project, 1997

If employee with a disability is treated similarly to employees without disabilities, concerning these elements of the employment process, the employee with a disability is more likely to be well integrated into the workplace:
• job acquisition process
• compensation
• work roles
• initial orientation and training

Better integration = higher hourly and monthly earnings

The longer someone is on the job does not lead to increases in:
• level of integration
• how typical employment experience is compared to others.
Therefore:
- integration needs to begin at day one
- from day one, employment experience needs to be as similar as possible to that of other employees

Co-worker vs. Agency support:
co-workers trained in providing support =
- more typical compensation
- higher hourly and monthly earnings
- higher participation in social activities with co-workers on and off the job
- more similar work roles

higher levels of agency support =
- lower wages
- lower levels of co-worker interaction

four or more hrs./wk. of agency support on job:
job is less likely to have
typical employment features

Exercise 7-A
Negotiating

Purpose: To practice thinking through the steps of negotiating with an employer and seeing the variety of strategies and styles used by fellow trainees.

Part I Instructions: Take ten minutes with a co-worker to strategize how you would approach meeting with an employer described in the situation below, using the scenario and questions listed. Then role play the scenario you discussed, acting as the job developer. After a few minutes, try a different scenario until you have tried a variety of styles and approaches.

You currently work with several people who have previous experience and current interest in retail work. Through a neighbor, you have managed to schedule an initial appointment with the manager of a local chain department store. The manager sounded hesitant on the phone but agreed to meet with you for fifteen minutes tomorrow morning. In small groups, plan out your strategy for what you will do in this meeting.

How will you start?

What will you present?

What questions will you ask?

What will you ask the manager to do?

On what note will you end?

What will you do next? And next? And next?

Part II Instructions: You've now had several meetings with the manager. The next step is to schedule the person for an interview. You have left several messages with the manager and she hasn't returned your call (which is unusual). You start to think that the manager is having second thoughts about working with you. Individually, take a few minutes to answer the following questions.

What strategies would you use to get in touch with the manager?

How could you find out what is really going on (assess the situation)?

Identify two possible reasons for the calls not being returned and suggest ways that you might alter your strategy to accommodate the needs/concerns of the manager.

Exercise 7-B
Placement Support Plan

Name: **Employer:**

What types of supports will the job seeker need following job placement? (Check all that apply.)

On-site support/job coaching

Regular contact with employer

Transportation assistance

Assistance with grooming and hygiene

Medication

Therapy

Reporting earnings to Social Security

Supervision during non-work hours

Communication with residential/family

Other

- Summary of support to be provided by employment agency:

- Summary of support to be provided by residential services:

- Summary of support to be provided by family:

- Summary of support to be provided by other resources (state funding agency, therapist, peers, employer, etc.):

What are the current support gaps and barriers?

What is the plan to overcome them?

Signatures of:

Job Seeker: **Agency Staff:**

Other(s) in support roles:

Date:

8

Identifying Employment Opportunities & Job Creation

This section explores guidelines for identifying employment opportunities for individuals who present a higher level of challenge. The focus is on identifying the specific assets that an individual has, and how these can be utilized to negotiate with an employer and identify a position that meets the needs of both the employer and the individual. An exercise provides experience and a format to follow in applying these concepts.

Successful job development for people with disabilities goes well beyond simply finding existing job openings and placing people in them. It is about meeting the specific and often unique needs of each individual. While job development in the nonprofit sector and particularly for people with disabilities at times has been portrayed as just a variation on personnel placement agencies, there is a major difference between the two.

Personnel agencies exist ultimately to meet the needs of the employer, and the clients they place are the means to meeting that need. Agencies that assist people with disabilities in finding employment have the needs of the job seeker as the primary focus. Meeting employer needs is simply the means to meeting those individual needs.

The Planning Process

When developing jobs for people with disabilities, start by determining the types of work environments and jobs that the individual desires, provide a good task/environment fit, and offer the greatest opportunity for long-term success. These factors should be considered in all job development. But the right environment is even more crucial for those people who don't fit easily into existing jobs or who will need extensive supports.

A focus on environment and task-match minimizes the need to "change the individual" or offer long-term job coaching. The better the fit with a person's skills and personality, the greater the likelihood of the worker's being valued and accepted on the job and the less need for extensive supports from the agency.

Job developers must creatively consider what attributes and skills the individual could potentially offer a business, and then analyze work environments to determine whether and how he or she could meet the needs of that business. Within the context of the job seeker's interests and abilities, begin the initial focus by establishing what type of work environments are a good fit for the individual and what specific tasks he or she could perform within that work environment. This forces the consideration of a good social fit (which is too often forgotten). It also can lead to more creative job development ideas.

WORK CULTURE AND SOCIAL INCLUSION

- Who works here?
- What supports are there from:
  - management?
  - other workers?
- Do people socialize?
  - on the job?
  - off the job?
- What are the social rules and norms?
- How much difference is:
  - allowed?
  - accepted?
  - appreciated?

As noted in Chapter 1, using a person-centered planning process that holistically considers an individual's interests, preferences, dislikes, and skills is an important element of job development for anyone with or without disabilities. This is particularly important for individuals who will require a high degree of creativity to find employment.

A quality person-centered planning process involves a variety of participants, uses effective brainstorming and networking, takes full advantage of existing relationships, and generates numerous ideas and real action. To maximize job search prospects, the contacts you develop through a person-centered planning process should be combined with those of staff and the agency. Developing opportunities, acceptance, and accommodations is much easier when there is a preexisting connection. Such "buy-in" and flexibility does not exist as readily with contacts made through cold-calling.

CREATIVE WORK OPTIONS

• Identify tasks, attributes, and interests.
• Identify environments: general and specific.
• Identify contacts.
• Identify supports.

Job Creation

While many employers initially may focus on existing needs, creating or "carving" jobs is a way of meeting employer demands while simultaneously meeting the employment needs of individuals who pose a particular marketing challenge. Job creation requires that the job developer or job seeker get the employer to view their personnel needs and ways of operating their business in more flexible ways then they have previously.

For example, the employer previously may not have hired people for only two hours per day, thinking it was unfeasible. However, the job developer may be working with someone for whom this would be perfect. This could be because the applicant has never worked in the past or he or she easily gets fatigued or cannot focus on a task for a long period of time.

A job developer can have success in creating jobs simply by catering to the needs readily identified by the employer. Another, more proactive, approach

is to help an employer recognize a need that they did not realize. (See job creation examples on page 75.)

Obviously, some employers are going to be more receptive to this approach than others. Be careful of the words you chose in gathering information and making proposals, to avoid the perception of telling the employer how they should be running their business. Some of the specific questions that can be asked of an employer to identify job creation possibilities include:

- Are there tasks that many employees do, which could be done by one individual?
- Are there tasks that take people away from critical tasks or their "real" jobs?
- Are there tasks that the employer would like employees to do better or more quickly?
- Are there tasks not getting done, because no one has the time?
- Are there times (during the day, week, or year) where extra help is needed?
- Are there jobs that are filled with students, high school students, or temporary workers? Would you like someone to fill those needs on a more stable basis?
- Does the employer have employees working overtime?
- If the employer asked employees what they wished they had help with, what would they say?
- Are there services that the employer has wanted to offer, but never had the resources?
- What is the biggest challenge the business faces in its day-to-day operations?
- What are the areas for growth or potential growth for the business?
- Are there services the business would like to offer that they are not presently?

Job creation requires gathering much information and ideas from an employer. You must have a solid relationship with an employer so they are willing to share such information and use more creative approaches to meeting personnel needs.

This can occur either through networking or by spending time with an employer prior to using this approach. This strategy often works after developing a relationship with employers through prior successful job matches.

• Networking and developing relationships are essential.
• You must meet an employer's perceived need.
• You should present in a way that is most similar to the employer's current situation.
• Give other examples, especially in the same type of business.
• Be willing to start on a trial basis or with less hours.
• Don't rush. It takes time to set up.
• Introduce the job seeker early in the process.

Specific examples of job creation include:

- A clerical support person in an office does filing, copying, opening of mail, and delivery of documents, so that higher paid administrative assistants and secretaries can concentrate on their assigned duties.
- An individual in the claims office of an insurance company opens all the claims that come in the mail and sorts them by type of claim, for processing by claims examiners.
- A restaurant, hotel, or food service operation that is extremely busy during the morning hours needs assistance with keeping supplies stocked, keeping the customer areas clean, and setting up coffee breaks.
- An individual in a large retail or warehouse operation collects and bales all cardboard.
- Business in a downtown area could use a new delivery service.

The greater the ability of the job developer to demonstrate to the employer the direct relationship between the created job and the perceived need that the employer has, the easier it will be to "sell" the employer. Suggestions for doing so include:

- pointing out to the employer the economic sense of paying someone to handle the more routine tasks and duties, instead of paying highly paid professional staff or using their own valuable time to perform such duties
- showing the manager or business owner how having someone take over tasks currently being done either haphazardly or not at all can increase efficiency, make their jobs easier, and give them time to concentrate on actual management and expansion of the business, rather than the daily operational details
- demonstrating how having a person with a disability perform the duties of a created job will increase customer satisfaction or staff efficiency, resulting in increased business (such as someone keeping a coffee station stocked and cleaned during peak hours at a food service establishment)
- for certain jobs and individuals, explaining to an employer how costly high turnover is, and how hiring a person with a disability can reduce turnover (Remember though, the reason some jobs are high turnover is that they are simply bad jobs that no one wants.)
- pointing out the costs involved in hiring temporary personnel from an agency, and how hiring a person with a disability instead can reduce those costs

A particularly advantageous way to sell an employer on job creation is to create a job that will pay for itself through higher sales or economic savings. An example of this is developing a delivery service component for a business that has not previously had such an option (such as a restaurant, deli, or video store). This can expand sales and pay for itself, particularly if there is an extra charge for delivery.

Another example is for an individual to break down old files or other items that are being discarded, saving and sorting the "usable" parts (like file folders and dividers). This reduces the employer's supply and disposal costs.

A third example is for a person with a disability to assist with the marketing efforts of a business. This can occur by handling a direct mail effort, or delivering door hangers or flyers to homes, cars, and businesses.

When meeting with an employer, a job developer may not immediately be able to identify opportunities for a job seeker. At the first meeting you simply may gather information from an employer. This gives you time to develop creative ideas away from the pressure of an employer meeting and to brainstorm creatively with fellow staff and job seekers based on the information gathered.

At the follow-up meeting, you can discuss and evaluate possible ideas. This also allows time to develop a stronger relationship with the employer. For more creative options, a formal written proposal that specifies the duties of the position and how it benefits the employer may be appropriate.

However, be careful about the message that such a formal proposal sends about the needs of people with disabilities. Anything done that deviates from the normal hiring process can create an aura that people with disabilities are in need of all sorts of extra help, assistance, and special treatment. It is important to remember that one of the underlying goals of helping people with disabilities gain employment is for each individual, according to his or her preferences, to be included and supported by mainstream society. Listed below are the essential elements of a proposal (written or verbal).

DEVELOPING A PROPOSAL

- The proposal must identify business need being meet.
- The benefits to the employer must be clear (e.g., financial savings, improved customer service).
- Employer and provider roles and responsibilities should be outlined.
- Remember the message that a written proposal sends:
  - formalizes the relationship between employer and agency
  - could potentially have a negative impact on the typical employer/employee relationship

There are some additional considerations to bear in mind when creating a job. Certain types of jobs, especially those related to food service, cleaning, and landscaping, have become "stereotypical" for people with disabilities. While these types of jobs will meet the needs of some people, service providers should move beyond these types of positions. It is also important not to be limited by the employer's available job openings, their vision of how tasks and jobs are organized, or the types of jobs currently existing within the workplace.

Present ideas in a way that respects the employer's way of doing business and business values. Also, any examples given from other businesses, particularly those that are similar, will help convince an employer to consider creating a position.

It would be an even stronger endorsement of this if other businesses would serve as a reference or even initiate a call to the potential employer in support of the agency. The job developer and job seeker also may have to be willing to start on a trial basis or with fewer hours in order to get the employer to agree to job creation. In this situation, continuing advocacy to expand the hours or scope of the job need to be a part of the extended support services provided by the agency.

Job creation, particularly the more creative options (such as developing a delivery business), can take an enormous amount of effort, energy, and time to implement. This is due to the time it takes to develop a relationship with an employer and negotiate specifics, make logistical arrangements, and provide additional support.

Therefore, job creation generally should be used with individuals for whom other options do not exist. Also, be careful of portraying people with disabilities as a "cheap" source of labor. For example, creating a clerical support position that pays slightly above minimum wage is a great opportunity for someone who has no previous work experience or who has worked only in minimum wage jobs. However, this is not a great opportunity if the person being placed in this position has extensive work experience, or if the employer is going to lay off employees who earn more because they have discovered this new source of "cheap labor." If "created" jobs are to last, they need to be real jobs that put the worker in a valued role in which the presence and work done by the worker produces benefits for the employer. Even with created jobs, integration on the job should occur, with the employer as the main source of support.

This can be more challenging with jobs that are not seen as a typical way of doing business if the agency is perceived as the source of the idea for the job. The employer may feel that since the agency came up with the idea for the job, it should provide the support to make it a reality. Finally, as with all job development, created jobs must be a good match with the individual needs, interests, and preferences of the job seeker.

These are the basic elements of job creation. Connecting the interests of an individual with an employer's needs requires good relationships built over time. Networking is a key strategy in building such connections. For individuals who pose a real challenge to your job development skills, these strategies are critical.

Exercise 8-A
Job Creation and Restructuring

Purpose: to practice systematically considering the needs of an individual and use this information to identify work environments and jobs in which the individual can be successful.

Instructions: Identify an individual you are currently trying to place. Try to pick an individual who poses a higher level of challenge, someone you may be experiencing difficulty in placing, or who does not fit readily into existing job openings. Develop a profile of the individual, including interests, accommodation needs, and the environments where he or she is happiest and most successful. Then get together in groups of five. One member of the group should share the information he or she has developed with the rest of the group. The group then should brainstorm to identify potential work environments and jobs in which this individual could be employed, using the questions in the exercise as a guide. Avoid the inclination to think about work environments first and the characteristics of the individual second. Instead, develop information about the individual first. Then, consider what types of jobs and work environments possibly could utilize the assets this individual has to offer. Brainstorm on as many individuals as time allows.

1) Begin by identifying an individual you work with, who presents a significant level of challenge in placement and may not fit readily into a preexisting job. Use the following outline to develop a short profile of the individual.

- Past experience (work, volunteer, school, life)

- Interests/Hobbies

- Tasks He or She Enjoys/Does Well
  (Remember to think about all areas of the person's life: home, present daytime activity, etc.)

- What kind of environments does he or she enjoy/fit in?

- Are there specific personality types with whom this individual is most comfortable or fits in well?

- Accommodation requirements

2) Brainstorm on possible work environments that might be a good setting for this person. Develop a list of at least four criteria for a work environment that would be a good match for each individual.

A.

B.

C.

D.

3) Identify at least one business that is potentially a good setting for each individual. For the purposes of this exercise, rely on your preexisting knowledge of this business. (In actual practice, you would go to the businesses you have identified and identify possible tasks or jobs for the person. Doing this would entail observation, talking to employees, managers, customers, and anyone else who may be a potential source of information.) Some of the questions to consider:

- What are the variety of tasks that are necessary for the business to operate?

- When is the business busiest: each day, during the week, during the year?

- Are there tasks that could be done more efficiently or more often?

- Are there tasks not getting done, because no one has the time?

- Are there tasks that take employees away from their more critical job duties (their areas of expertise or "real" jobs)?

- Does the employer have employees working overtime?

- If the business and employees could have help with anything, what would it be?

- What is the biggest challenge the business faces in its day-to-day operations?

- What are the areas for growth or potential growth for the business?

- Are there services the business would like to offer that it is not doing presently?

- Summarize the type of work atmosphere and culture.

4) From the information developed in #3, put together a list of tasks, jobs, and areas in which the individual you profiled could potentially meet an employer need. Include any possible accommodation needs that might be helpful to ensure the individual's success.

9

Customer Service and On-Going Relationships

In a perfect world, a job developer could walk into a business with an appointment and secure a job for an individual. The reality is that business needs vary over time due to a wide variety of factors: employee turnover, expansion, and retraction; the vagaries of the economy; change in management; and the morale of the business. As noted earlier, it also takes time to build a relationship and a level of mutual trust (particularly with larger employers). Such trust often is needed when you help individuals with more significant levels of disability get jobs.

Building a relationship with employers does not end when an individual gets a job. Continuing to work at the relationship is beneficial for:

- keeping the communication lines open to proactively address any issues that may arise
- advocating for the employee's support needs and career growth
- staying aware of trends and changes within the business
- identifying additional openings for other individuals

Even if an employer has fired an individual, maintaining that relationship might be advantageous in order to pave the way for future placements. One of the main reasons for working at relationships with employers (those who hire, those who don't hire, and those who fire) is that businesses know other businesses. If an employer thinks highly of a job developer and his or her agency, the employer may both hire other job applicants and recommend the agency to other employers.

On the other hand, the employer who is left with bad feelings passes that message along to other businesses. This may increase the apprehension a new employer already may have about hiring a worker with a disability.

Treating customers well is a trademark of successful businesses such as Nordstrom, Marriott, and Disney Corporation. These businesses have found that treating the customer well translates directly into repeat business, good public relations, and, most importantly, increased sales and profits.

Good customer service may be a concept that seems more at home with a restaurant or retail store than with programs that provide employment services for people with disabilities. However, as with any other business, quality customer service is key to successfully helping people with disabilities become employed. It is not as clear in community employment agencies exactly who is the customer that must be served.

In the private sector, the customer is the person who pays for the goods or services. In employment services, there are a number of individuals and entities that must be satisfied including: the job seeker, the employer, family members, funding agencies, and the agency that employs the job developer. While there may seem to be a number of different customers who must be equally satisfied, the authors believe there is only <u>one</u> customer whose needs are the priority: *the job seeker with a disability*.

These other stakeholders are important and a good job developer makes the effort to find out their needs and respond to them. A customer service approach is used to develop the involvement and support of these parties in order to achieve successful employment outcomes for the job seeker. However, it is the job seeker's interests and needs that must guide this process and meeting those needs must be the ultimate goal.

In particular, employers are critical stakeholders (or secondary customers) whose needs must be met in order to successfully assist the job seeker to become employed. Treat employers well, and spend time and effort to ensure that employers are satisfied with both the worker and services.

Meeting employers' needs is part of the process – a very necessary part of helping job applicants get and maintain employment. However, being nice to employers and having them perceive the job developer/agency in a positive manner is not the ultimate outcome – getting people employed is.

This distinction can be illustrated best by examples of how one can meet the employer's needs but not meet the needs of the primary customer, the job seeker. In the first example, a job developer can choose to screen out workers who have any sort of behavioral problems and refer only "sure bets" to a local employer. The employer will be happy, but this won't provide services to the people who need services the most.

A contrasting situation is where the job developer has made a commitment to an employer to fill a job in a tight labor market. Yet, the job is not really a good job match for any of the individuals he or she represents. Does the job developer persuade the applicant to take the job anyway?

WHY MAINTAIN ONGOING EMPLOYER RELATIONSHIPS

It is important to continue to work at a relationship with an employer, even after a job has been developed, for a variety of reasons:
• You're being proactive, which keeps communication lines open.
• It is "money in the bank" for future concerns and support needs.
• The employer possibly may be able to hire other individuals in the future.
• The employer can be a source of job leads.
• The employer can act as reference for other employers.

Another example is when an employer calls to say that the company is having difficulty with a particular worker the agency helped get a job and they want help letting the person go. The job developer believes that the company has not provided adequate training or support, or maybe has dealt with the worker in a discriminatory manner. Does the job developer keep up good relations with the employer and help them get the person out of there quickly at the expense of that worker? Or does he

or she advocate for the worker, potentially causing problems in the relations with that employer?

Obviously, the ideal situation is one in which both the worker's and the employer's needs are met, but the real world does not always yield win-win propositions. The crucial question is: When needs conflict, whose needs are sacrificed, and at what cost?

What does taking a customer service approach with employers mean? On a basic level, it means treating people with courtesy and respect, such as: being on time for appointments, greeting them with a smile, answering the phone in a polite and professional manner, returning phone calls promptly, writing thank-you notes, and performing the other niceties of life that all too often are taken for granted.

It entails being sensitive to an employer's schedule and business responsibilities. It means asking employers if it is a good time to talk, and if not, rescheduling at their convenience. It requires having enough business (and common) sense not to call on a food service manager at 11:30 in the morning when lunch is about to be served or try to schedule a meeting with the manager of an accounting firm during the first two weeks in April.

CUSTOMER SERVICE TENETS

• Know who your customer is. (Employer relations is a strategy, not the goal.)
• Produce results. (Good intentions are not enough.)
• Take care of details.
• Cater to self-identified, not assessed needs.
• Under-promise, over-deliver.
• Offer assistance, not information.
• Show respect, politeness, honesty, and enthusiasm.
• No complaints? No feedback? Worry!
• Handle complaints quickly.
• Add the personal touch.
• Recognize and reward.

Good customer service involves finding out what employers want and need and responding accordingly. This goes well beyond saying, "Call me if there's a problem." A key to customer service is keeping the communication lines open with consistent contact in order to develop an awareness of the situation early enough and create a level of comfort among those involved.

Many job developers say they wish employers would call so they could help with difficult situations, but in reality the responsibility should not rest solely with the employer. It is the job developer's responsibility to reach out to employers and create opportunities for them to explain their needs as a business, what's wrong as well as what's right.

In mainstream American culture, it is typical to be reticent with people you don't know particularly well and more open with people who are more familiar. It is easier to be more honest and blunt with good friends than with new acquaintances. To provide good customer service, you need to get beyond the cursory acquaintance stage with people and create real avenues of communication.

This means getting to know each employer's preferences and idiosyncrasies and dealing with them accordingly. For example, you may drop in on some employers unexpectedly and chitchat for fifteen minutes about sports or upcoming vacations or share stories about his or her kids or pets. With other employers, it is important to call ahead and set up formal meetings that are strictly business oriented.

SERVICE IN A CORPORATE CULTURE

- Remember you're an outsider.
- Respect people's time.
- Stay informed about company issues.
- Keep it simple.
- Always get permission.
- Keep communicating.
- Assume responsibility for mistakes.
- Keep learning about the company.

Once you have established a good relationship with an employer and dealt with and solved problematic situations, you then can expect the employer to take at least some of the initiative to call if another problem arises (though some level of consistent contact is still advisable). With a new employer, it is better to err on the side of caution and expect to initiate communication. As with any dealings with employers, a job developer will need to customize his or her approach to the particular personality and style of each employer.

Part of good communication also means being easy to reach. This means that employers (along with the job applicant and other stakeholders) should know how to find the job developer via his or her office, beeper, etc. Whoever answers the phone at the agency would know how to deal professionally with the caller.

What happens when people call the agency? Are they greeted warmly, made to feel their call is welcome, and responded to quickly? Or, are they treated as if the call is an inconvenience or burden to the person answering the phone? Is the person answering the phone able to provide information or respond to a given situation in a helpful manner? Or is the person unhelpful or even rude? If that's the case, then this needs to be address internally, or the job developer will need to figure out an alternate way of forwarding messages such as getting a cellular phone, beeper, or voice mail.

Beyond good manners and social skills, good customer service ultimately means helping job seekers get and stay employed, with the focus on job seeker and employer satisfaction. It means having a sense of priorities.

For example, if you are working on a report that is due the next day and an employer calls because a worker is experiencing performance problems, good customer service means making the employer feel glad he or she called. It means not indicating in any way that the call is an inconvenience. When an employer calls at a bad time, it might be tempting to mention the other demands on your time, but instead make sure that you communicate that the employer's call is welcome.

If you cannot respond at that time, offer to get back in touch later that day or find someone else who can help right away. Good customer service also means listening and responding to the employer's concerns while advocating for the employee. Depending on the nature of the situation, this may include going over to the job site that day. Bear in mind, though, that the presence of a professional on the job site is not always necessary or desirable for every problem that occurs.

A balance between assertive outreach and persistence in doing sales and marketing is crucial. So is a customer service/relationship-building approach. It's important to be aggressive, but avoid pushing too hard. For staff who are new or uncomfortable with job development, knowing when and how to be assertive with employers is particularly difficult. The tendency is to be afraid to call back or ask for something for fear of alienating the employer. Some suggestions to help job developers find a comfortable way of being assertive without being a pest are below.

While being responsive to the concerns of the employer in such a situation, again remember that the real customer is the person with a disability. It is crucial to be cautious of automatic total agreement and acquiescence to whatever the employer is saying.

Customer Service: The Key to Good Follow-Up

Providing good customer service is key to developing long-term relationships with employers. Being responsive, being conscious of one's role as an outsider, and showing basic common courtesies and social graces (such as the often overlooked task of writing thank-you letters) are all key.

But there are additional strategies to use both as a way to follow-up with employers and build relationships. These include inviting the employer to be a member of the Employer Advisory Board/Business Advisory Council, using the employer for informational and mock interviews, asking for employer advice on marketing materials, and sending the employer articles of interest. It is important to use a variety of methods and adapt them to the individual employer.

The goal in using a variety of strategies to build a relationship is to enable the employer to learn about all the positive things the agency has to offer. More important is providing the organization an opportunity to learn about people with disabilities as individuals and how they can be an asset to an employer.

Having a variety of ways to expose employers to agencies and people with disabilities, without their having to hire an applicant right away, allows for the time to build the relationship and establish credibility. This increases the chances of a hire at a later date. While using a variety of methods is helpful, the most important thing is to maintain regular contact and use some type of system to ensure that contact occurs regularly.

FOLLOWING-UP

• Have employer files.
• Have a system for tracking follow-up: calendar, tickler file, and marketing software.
• Record specific information: names, potential needs, interests, and idiosyncrasies.
• Decide how often you should follow-up.
• Vary your follow-up methods.
• Don't expect employers to call you; you make the call.

Follow-up often breaks down simply because there is not a systematic way of making sure it happens. Every good salesperson has some way of keeping track of the contacts that have been made and ensuring that regular follow-up occurs. The same should be true of job developers.

Methods can range from simply writing reminders in a daily diary, to manual tickler file card systems, to high-tech marketing software. The important thing is to ensure regular follow-up. Record personal information about the employer such as interests and idiosyncrasies in order to individualize communication with the employer.

Instead of inventing a system, you can learn from businesses about the follow-up tracking systems they use for their sales people, and find one with which you are comfortable.

PURPOSE OF EMPLOYER DATA COLLECTION

• documenting employer information (name, address, contact person, etc.)
• tracking job leads
• managing follow-up with employers
• providing a central data base accessible to all
• managing the job development process through tracking of activity
• ensuring accountability and goal setting in job development

EMPLOYER INFORMATION TO GATHER

- the basics - employer name, address, contact people
- employer idiosyncrasies
- type of business/jobs
- source of job lead
- frequency of contact
- type of contact – phone, in-person, etc.
- job seeker interviews generated
- jobs developed

WHAT TO KEEP TRACK OF

- number of new leads
- summary sources of new leads
- number and type (phone, in-person, etc.) of initial and follow-up contacts
- number of job seeker interviews
- number of jobs developed
- types of jobs developed
- track information by program and staff member
- totals and averages
- provide accountability for program and staff
- set program and staff goals
- identify trends

With the pressures to get people quickly placed, job developers tend to concentrate on businesses with immediate openings and placing the "easy" job seekers. If you are going to place with "nontraditional" employers and place individuals with the most significant disabilities in community employment, the ability to develop long-term relationships is essential.

An example of this is recent research on placement of individuals with disabilities in white collar jobs that the President's Committee on Employment of People with Mental Retardation has conducted. Findings show that it often takes a minimum of six months to a year of relationship-building before a placement occurs.[8]

Since a job developer's time is valuable, decide whether continuing to invest time in developing a relationship is worthwhile, or if the time would be better spent pursuing other leads. The ultimate question is, *"Will further investment of time and energy potentially result in the development of a job?"*

Sometimes it is necessary to discontinue follow-up for a while and try again later, when conditions are more favorable (such as when a new manager is hired or economic conditions improve). Any consistent follow-up is better than none. The more the methods involve the employer, the better. Much of marketing in the private sector is intended to increase name recognition. The goal of follow-up for job development is the same: to remind employers on a consistent basis of the agency as a potential source of good employees.

Using the follow-up methods discussed in this section is particularly important for people to gain jobs in nontraditional settings or with larger employers, or for finding jobs for people with the most significant level of disability. These situations all require building long-term relationships with employers.

KEEPING EMPLOYERS INVOLVED

- Be a resource on the ADA.
- Provide consultation on accommodations needed to make the workplace accessible for employees and customers.
- Provide consultation on accommodation needs for current employees with disabilities.
- Use the employer as an assessment site (job tryout, job sampling).
- Use the employer for mock interviews to give job seekers practice in interviewing.
- Use the employer for workplace tours for job seekers to learn about different employment options.
- Have the employer join your business advisory council/employment advisory board.
- Use thank-you and follow-up letters.
- Send out holiday cards.
- Send the employer your newsletter.
- Provide recognition and rewards.
- Have the employer help develop/review your marketing materials.
- Have the employer assist and provide feedback in development of marketing presentations.
- Get employer assistance in development of a job development tracking system.

Exercise 9-A
Customer Service Tenets

Purpose: To promote consideration and discussion of the principles of good customer service.

Instructions: In small groups, come up with six to ten basic principles or tenets that could serve as guidelines for a customer service approach with employers. Consider not only the way that you conduct business with employers, but also the interactions that other personnel in your agency have with these individuals.

1.

2.

3.

4.

5.

6.

7.

8.

9.

10.

Exercise 9-B
Case Study: Customer
Service in Job Development

Purpose: To give an example of using customer service when approaching a prospective employer.

Instructions: Read the exercise below, which is based on an actual event.

A food service manager needs to hire a food preparation person to make sandwiches and salads for a cafeteria operation in a 600-person office building. He runs an advertisement in the local paper. The ad is seen by a job developer for an agency that provides employment services to people with disabilities. The job developer calls the number in the ad, and talks to the food service manager. The conversation goes as follows:

Job Developer: This is Madeline Jones from XYZ Services. I work with people with disabilities. I saw your ad in the paper for the food preparation person. I have a woman who I am trying to find a job for, and I would like to know if you would consider her for this position.

Manager: You know, I would really love to do something like this, but I don't see how it would work. I'm very busy and the place is somewhat chaotic. We also work in pretty tight quarters. I just don't see how it would work.

Job Developer: She really needs a job. Would you <u>please</u> consider hiring her?

Manager: As I said, I'd really like to be involved in something like this, but I don't see it working.

Job Developer: Could I at least send you a brochure on our program?

Manager: Sure, no problem. (He gives the job developer the address, and they exchange good-bye pleasantries.)

The manager receives the brochure in the mail a few days later. He puts the brochure in his desk, where it sits until he moves out of the office three years later.

What went wrong in this situation? What could have been handled better? If you were the job developer, is there anything you would have done differently? Specifically outline the steps you would have taken.

In hindsight, it is always easy to see what should have been done. However, when uncomfortable or new at job development, one often says or does things that in retrospect are not ideal. One of the most common mistakes is for the job developer to spend too much time talking and presenting lots of information about the job seeker, the program, and the services. Instead, the job developer should be listening to the employer to find out as much as possible and asking questions to elicit more information. This way, he or she can present information that is targeted to that particular employer's wants, needs, and concerns.

10

Time Management and Professional Development

This section examines two priority areas for job developers: the amount of time it takes to do effective job development and the importance of professional development. It discusses ways to set job development goals and looks at a variety of strategies to effectively plan for and implement job development time in the daily and weekly schedule. These strategies address both steps you personally can take to use your time more effectively and areas to discuss with supervisors or agencies regarding your role and responsibilities. Also, it reviews how to develop a personal professional development plan that will enhance your skills and abilities.

Time Management

There are two keys to success in job development to meet the needs of people with disabilities. One is having the skills to do it, which has been the main focus of this book. The other key, though, is simply devoting enough time to the process, "pounding the pavement." You can be the most highly skilled job developer in the world, with the ability to "talk a dog off a meat truck." But if you do not devote sufficient time to job development, people with disabilities are not going to get jobs.

Generally most vocational services staff simply don't spend enough time doing job development to meet the needs of individuals served by the program or agency. This may be due to many factors such as fear or dislike of job development or competing agency priorities. But even staff who enjoy and value job development have difficulty setting aside the necessary time to do it effectively.

WHAT DOES IT TAKE?

The following figures will vary based on factors including the number of cold versus warm or networking contacts, job seeker skills and experiences, type of job, agency and individual experience, community connections/ reputation, economic conditions, and transportation access.

10 - 20 cold calls = 1 interview

7 - 10 interviews = 1 job

Many of the job responsibilities of community employment staff are driven by the immediate needs and demands of individuals with disabilities, employers, families, other staff, and service providers. On the other hand, job development is primarily a proactive rather than reactive activity and requires different skills and behaviors to be done effectively.

Before any tangible results are seen, the job developer first must plan out and take a variety of steps (phone calls, visits, follow-up, etc.). You need to plan, coordinate, and follow up on many individual activities over weeks, and even months, without any outside impetus or concrete reward for the effort. Unless employment staff make a conscious and dedicated effort to schedule time to do job development, it is easy for other activities to take priority.

By the same token, it is important that employment staff receive the support from their supervisor and agency to afford them the time to do job development effectively. Proactive planning should include examining the various activities that make up your job.

Ask yourself how each activity is connected with helping someone with a disability find and keep a job. If there is no connection, then some thought and discussion should take place as to whether that activity should be assigned to someone else, made a low priority to be done when time is available, or eliminated entirely.

In a study of thirteen agencies in Massachusetts, community employment staff whose jobs included job development responsibilities spent an average of 4% to 8% of their time on job development.[9] This was insufficient time to develop the quantity and quality of job opportunities wanted and needed by individuals served by their agencies.

Human service staff often have the best of intentions when it comes to job development. However, the setting of clear, measurable job development goals, which staff are then held accountable for, ensures that sufficient time and energy will be devoted to job development.

Job seekers with disabilities will get jobs only if adequate time is devoted to job development. For this to happen, job developers must take responsibility for how they spend their time, whether this means making changes themselves or negotiating with others in the agency to bring about the needed modifications.

Part of time management for a job developer also is ensuring that there is maximum involvement of others in the job development process, so that the job developer is not solely responsible for all job development activities. Is the job seeker, his or her family and friends, residential staff, and other agency staff generating ideas, making contacts, providing assistance, and doing their part? Could they do more?

YEARLY HIRING GOALS

50 placements = 400 interviews = 5000 company contacts

Job development requires goals. Think about how the goals listed compare to your current job development activities. It is easy to feel overwhelmed when you look at the raw numbers of what it takes to do job development.

It is important to remember that this information substantiates what a large task job development is, and illustrates the need for devoting planned time. This information can be used to advocate within an agency for the needed structure, resources, job design, and supports for sufficient job development activity.

Over 90% of job development is proactive. It is often very easy to put off these activities, unless you set goals and plan time accordingly. Listed above right are tips for devoting more time and effectively using time to help people find jobs.

Two additional time management suggestions are:
1) accounting for travel time in planning
2) improving the communication system among staff to avoid writing and repeating the same information

MANAGING YOUR TIME: STRATEGIES FOR PRIORITIZING JOB DEVELOPMENT

- Schedule phone time daily.
- Contact a certain number of employers each day/week.
- Call back persistently (one to three days).
- Use an employer contact log/tickler file.
- Schedule blocks of time for marketing and direct employer contacts in the community.
- Develop a specific marketing/job development plan for each person, with timelines.
- Have a general marketing plan and goals with weekly and monthly goals.
- Schedule meetings on Fridays and lunch times.
- Schedule employer meetings and other marketing activities on your way to and from home.
- Use a laptop computer and cellular phone.
- Use beeper, voice, and e-mail effectively.
- Learn to say no.

Professional Development

Finding jobs for people with disabilities goes beyond just helping people get a paycheck. It is also about enabling people to have opportunities for growth and learning in their lives. People who are responsible for developing jobs for people with disabilities also need the same growth and learning opportunities.

To continue to succeed in human services and as a job developer, it is important to pursue ongoing professional development. In any profession, if you do not regularly look for ways to improve how you do a job, and never venture outside the confines of the specific job responsibilities, it is easy to become complacent. There are plenty of people in a variety of fields who were once the "star performers," or at least reasonably competent, whose performance has gradually diminished because they have not changed with the times or developed new skills.

Paying attention to professional development is preventive medicine against becoming complacent, and possibly unemployed. You can look for better ways to do the job, keep skills sharp, share knowledge with other professionals, and learn new ideas or at least refresh old ones.

If human services were a stagnant field, professional development would be important simply to maintain skills and enthusiasm for the job. However, like most fields, human services is in a constant state of change. Many people who were once considered "unemployable" are now working successfully in the community as a result of such innovations as supported employment and assistive technology. The number of individuals for whom community employment is an option is continuing to grow.

The field of employment for people with disabilities needs to continue to seek out new strategies so that employment in the community is a possibility for all people with disabilities. At the same time, the continual high unemployment rates for people with disabilities indicates that no one entity or person is doing such a great job that there isn't more for everyone to learn and things that could be done better.

It is important for anyone in any field to pay attention to his or her professional development for personal gain and career growth. In this field, the people served are counting on the professionals to be as dedicated, innovative, and skilled as possible. Therefore, it is paramount that those working in the disability field, including job developers, make every effort to ensure that they maintain their professional dedication, remain up-to-date on the latest developments in the field, and try new and different strategies.

Professional development can occur through a variety of means. A major part of professional development is simply looking for ways to improve performance on a day-to-day basis. It is important to be confident about how to do things (particularly something like job development). But it's also important to keep egos in check, question how to do better, and engage in some self-analysis about improving the quality of work and yielding better outcomes.

In addition to looking for ways to enhance performance in day-to-day activities, professional development also means getting beyond the confines of daily routines for professional enrichment. Some of the more obvious ones are attending training for professionals and participating in professional associations.

Others include taking courses at a local college or university. Simply reading a book or articles in a professional journal can provide new thoughts and ideas. Professional development also can occur by trying new ideas and strategies at work or becoming involved in special projects with other people in the organization.

Some of the best professional development can occur by getting outside the human service world. Taking courses in marketing and presentations or getting involved in a local business association can provide opportunities not only for professional development, but also for job development contacts.

In the ideal world, everyone would work for organizations that value professional development and encourage the pursuit of such opportunities. But organizations vary their focus on professional development, with emphasis all too often on the here and now rather than the long-term. It is important that individual staff seek out opportunities for professional development and advocate within their organization for the necessary resources (such as fees for training or simply time to participate in such activities or try new strategies).

If you desire professional development opportunities outside the normal discipline, it is important to point out to your supervisor how such opportunities are not just of personal benefit to the employee, but also to the organization and ultimately the people served by the organization. If the organization simply does not value professional development, then individuals should seek out such opportunities on their own, during their own time. Such opportunities can be pursued at little or no cost. Even if the organization does not value professional growth, every individual should value it to grow in his or her career and do the best job possible in meeting the needs of people with disabilities.

Professional development essentially requires that one pushes oneself beyond the normal level of comfort. To grow professionally and personally, we need to do things differently. We need to do things that professionals are not necessarily very good at (at least initially) and things that require individuals to make mistakes and learn. We need to put ourselves in situations and environments in which we are not necessarily comfortable. Job developers constantly are asking people with disabilities to do this. We should require the same of ourselves.

This book has provided a comprehensive overview of the various aspects of job development for people with disabilities. However, attending all the trainings and reading all the books that exist on job development are not going to automatically turn an individual into a competent and expert job developer.

SKILL ENHANCEMENT STRATEGIES

- Take additional training, both human service and other types.
- Join and be active in professional groups, both disability and non-disability (business).
- Join and be active in civic organizations and clubs and community affairs.
- Take college and adult education classes in marketing and related topics.
- Take a public speaking course or join a public speaking group.
- Obtain marketing training from businesses.
- Read books and journals, both disability and non-disability related.
- Read the business section of your newspaper and local business magazines and newspapers.

Training provides a good basis for becoming an expert job developer, but experience is the best teacher. The only way to become really proficient at job development is to actually get out there and do it. Job developers need to feel a sense of urgency about what they do on a daily basis, as if someone's life depends on their ability to do their job well. In reality, someone's life does depend on it – the person with a disability.

If an individual is hesitant or really struggling with job development, here are some ideas on how to overcome these barriers:

- Pair up with someone who is a good job developer. Learn how they develop contacts. Go with them to presentations and meetings. Have them be a mentor and provide feedback. Absorb what they do and then incorporate it into the your style, making it your own.
- Don't become overwhelmed by the seemingly large task of finding someone a job. You can break down the process in your mind and set short-term goals (e.g., "I want to make ten job contacts today," "My goal is to set up three meetings with employers.")

- Do some mock presentation and interactions with co-workers. Once you are feeling a little confident, do mock presentations and interactions with business people and employers. Videotape and critique these sessions.

Here are some other ideas to consider to increase your professional development and provide better service:

1. Getting to Know the Job Seeker

- Focus less on disability and medical information.
- Spend time with the job seeker in different settings
- Find out about the person's interests, hobbies and family, and how he or she spends time.
- Establish a focus on areas of interest.
- Develop a standard placement planning format that includes: background information, tasks/jobs the person is interested in, positive attributes, possible places to look, accommodations and support needs, and a plan of action.
- Hold a planning/brainstorming session that includes the person, family members, friends, and other individuals important to him or her.
- If interests and skills are not clear, set up a series of situational assessments in work settings.

2. Presenting Job Seeker

- Develop a way to talk about the person without using medical or rehabilitation jargon.
- Develop a list of the job seeker's strengths, interests, skills, and assets.
- Develop a resume/personal profile that highlights the individual's positive attributes.
- If a disability is obvious, determine how to talk about it.
- Obtain information on sources and resources for assistive technology.
- Prepare ways to discuss accommodations.
- Identify ways to present the individual and your services to create a socially inclusive environment and enhance natural supports.
- Use many different styles – avoid the "one size fits all" approach.

3. Making Contacts

- Determine a list of sources for research information.
- Do research on your local economy and specific businesses.
- Map out your own personal network, and use those contacts.
- Map out the job seeker's network, and use those contacts.
- Develop a phone script and test it out on people you know.
- Join and become active in business and community groups.
- Develop a standard data collection method to measure actions:
  - # of phone calls/initial contacts per day/week/month.
  - # of follow-up calls per day/week/month.
  - # of tours taken.

4. Social Skills

- Do a self-examination of your style/first impressions.
- Have other individuals observe your style and get feedback on your approach.
- Practice different approaches and styles.
- Keep your style fresh. Don't get stagnant. Keep growing.
- Videotape and critique your presentation style by yourself or with others.

5. Customer Service

- Develop a variety of ways to remain in contact over the long-term such as: using employers for mock interviews and assessment, membership on a Business Advisory Council, providing consultation and training on disability issues, letters, phone calls, and a newsletter.
- Develop methods for ensuring regular follow-up contact with employers (calendars, computer software, etc.).
- Measure actions weekly.

6. Making the Deal

- Develop methods for negotiating with employers so that job seekers receive equal treatment, respect, and acceptance.
- Determine methods for negotiating with employers that ensures support comes mainly from sources other than paid staff of the service provider.
- Determine what should be offered to employers "up front" and what should be "sweeteners" and "hole cards."
- Obtain information on financial incentives such as OJT funds and ADA tax credits.

7. Marketing Materials

- Have a number of businesses review your materials, and get feedback.
- Update all materials regularly.

Exercise 10-A
Managing Your Time

Purpose: To help job developers apply the information discussed in this chapter by identifying specific ways to change work habits to: 1) devote more time to job development; 2) use job development time more effectively.

Instructions: Identify below two or three job development activities you would like to do (or do more of). Then list two or three non-job-development activities you plan to reduce or eliminate to increase your time spent on job development. Making job development a priority must include both doing more job development and doing other activities less or differently. Just adding more activities to an already full workload will result in lack of follow-through with job development. Please be specific about the time, (i.e., particular day and number of hours) you will devote to additional job development and reduce other activities. If you find yourself in a situation in which you don't have enough time to do any parts of your job adequately because your job responsibilities are so great or diverse, even the best time management won't be effective. In this case, it will be necessary to sit down with your supervisor and others in your agency to discuss roles, responsibilities, priorities, and workload and come to some mutual agreement. In doing so though, you should have clear documentation about how your time is currently being spent and a clear sense of the amount of time it will require to meet the job development needs of the people served by the agency. You also should offer strategies on how other agency staff, consumers, families, and residential managers could potentially better support the job development process.

Identify two to three specific job development activities you plan to do (or do more of) on a weekly basis during the next thirty days. Identify the number of hours you plan to devote weekly and when.

Activity   # Hours   When

Identify two to three specific activities that you plan to do less of, differently, or stop doing on a weekly basis to make time to do more job development during the next thirty days. Identify when these activities occur and the number of hours redirected to job development.

Activity   When   # Hours Saved

Exercise 10-B:
Designing a Professional
Development Plan

Purpose: To understand the importance of ongoing professional development and design a list of methods and resources for professional development, to help apply the information and ideas in this book.

Instructions: Fully benefiting from the information presented in this manual will happen only if you determine ways of applying the information to your day-to-day activities. In your job, you should have specific ideas about what to do differently, how to continue to expand your knowledge of the field, and how to make professional development a continuous part of what you do. Continuous innovation and dedication to improving knowledge is essential, particularly in a field that is constantly evolving and that also has a long way to go before it truly fulfills the employment needs of all people with disabilities.

Come up with three ideas to enhance your abilities as a professional. Fill out the *Professional Development Plan* form on the next page with ideas, documenting how to accomplish these items.

Choose ideas that will enhance day-to-day performance and others that will provide enrichment (such as taking a class or joining a community group). It is also important to pick at least one idea that forces you to do things in a different way from the usual approach. This possibly could put you in situations that push you to overcome some personal barriers and fears.

• What professional development activities do you currently participate in?

• Are there resources available or that you are using that may be of help to others?

• What community activities are you involved with?

• What are some good materials or methods you have found for research on businesses?

• What books, journal articles, or other materials have you found particularly helpful?

• What has been key to your success as a job developer?

Professional Development Plan

Name: _____ **Date:** _____

• I feel my strengths as a job developer are:

• I feel the areas in which I could improve to be an even <u>better</u> job developer are:

• The following are three things I will do so that I will be the best job developer I can be:

1. What I will do:

How I will do it:

Resources I will need:

Date for completion:

2. What I will do:

How I will do it:

Resources I will need:

Date for completion:

3. What I will do:

How I will do it:

Resources I will need:

Date for completion:

Exercise 10-C
Using Your Network

Purpose: To practice the development of job contacts using the concept of networking through personal and professional connections.

Instructions: Develop a list of people you could contact to explore possible jobs in the field of your choice. All people on the list need to be people whom you know or can contact through someone you know. When you have completed your list, count the number of contacts generated for the assignment and record the number. Either in person or by phone, contact at least one of the individuals on your list to discuss potential positions. Then answer the following questions:

How did you go about developing your list of contacts? Who did you include?

Are there others now that come to mind for potential contacts?

How did you decide which contact you actually were going to call or talk to?

How did you approach that conversation?

What were the results of this call?

Were there any helpful suggestions made by your contact?

Is there anything you would do differently if you were to try this again?

Did you have a difficult time thinking of contacts?

Did you feel uncomfortable, or reluctant, in doing the assignment?

Do you have any advice for someone struggling to reach out to his or her own contacts?

Exercise 10-D
What Do I Say?

Purpose: To spend time working on the actual wording for a future interaction with an employer.

Instructions: Develop a script for a phone call or walk-in for an opening with an employer you don't know. There is a specific applicant in mind for the job. Be prepared to present your script during the next day of training. Try to engage the employer and not just talk nonstop for the first minute. Work many questions for the employer to answer into the script/presentation.

About the Authors

Cecilia Gandolfo, M.S.Ed., has over eighteen years in the rehabilitation and special education fields. She is a lead training associate at the Institute for Community Inclusion at Children's Hospital in Boston. Her background includes experience as a teacher, employment training specialist, consultant, and co-owner of a private for-profit rehabilitation agency. At the institute her responsibilities include developing, coordinating, and leading workshops related to employment for persons with disabilities. She has presented on both a local and national basis.

Martine E. Gold, M.S., is the director of transitional services at Challenge Industries in Ithaca, New York, and is also a consultant to the Program on Employment and Disability at Cornell University. She has almost twenty-five years of experience in human services in a variety of direct service, consulting, and management roles, with extensive experience in job development. She has done training and technical assistance on employment throughout the US, with a great deal of focus on organizational change.

David Hoff, M.S.W., is a lead training associate at the Institute for Community Inclusion at Children's Hospital in Boston. He provides training and technical assistance on a variety of issues related to the employment of people with disabilities. He is the co-author of several articles and manuals related to the issue of employment of people with disabilities, and has presented at numerous local and national conferences. His background includes extensive experience directly assisting people with disabilities to find and maintain employment, as well managerial positions in the private sector.

Melanie Jordan, B.S., has over twenty years of diverse human service experience. She is currently a training associate with the Institute for Community Inclusion at Children's Hospital in Boston. Prior to her current involvement in training and staff development, her work with people with disabilities around employment-related issues included job development, job coaching, and case management. Her advocacy efforts also have included work in special education, residential services, family support intervention, and elder protective services.

References

[1]"Employer Survey Assesses Use of Search/Placement," *The Fordyce Letter*. December 1996, pp. 1-7.

[2]Johnston, W. and Packer, A., *Workforce 2000: Work and Workers for the Twenty-First Century*. Indianapolis: Hudson Institute, 1987.

[3]Bortnic, S. and Ports, M., "Job Search Methods and Results: Tracking the Unemployed," *Monthly Labor Review*. US Department of Labor, December 1992, pp. 29-35.

[4]Temelini, D. and Fesko, S., "Shared Responsibility: Job Search Practices from the Consumer and Staff Perspective," *Research to Practice,* Institute for Community Inclusion, June, 1996.

[5]Pitt-Catsouphes, M., Litchfield, L., and Lilly, T., *What Matters? Workplace Responses to Employees with Disabilities*. Boston: Center on Promoting Employment - RRTC, 1998.

[6]Galloway, C., *Employers as Partners: A Guide to Negotiating Jobs for People with Disabilities*. Sonoma, CA: California Institute on Human Services, 1982.

[7]Mank, D., Cioffi, A., and Yovanoff, P., "Analysis of the Typicalness of Supported Employment Jobs, Natural Supports, and Wage and Integration Outcomes," *Mental Retardation*. Vol. 35, No. 3, 1997, pp. 185-197.

[8]Raggio, C., *White Collar Employment Opportunities for People with Cognitive Disabilities*. President's Committee on the Employment of People with Disabilities, 1997.

[9]Gold, M., Van Gelder, M., and Schalock, R., "A Behavioral Approach to Understanding and Managing Organizational Change: Moving from Workshops to Community Employment," *Journal of Rehabilitation Administration*. Vol. 22, No. 3, 1999, pp. 191-207.